Barbecue
& More

CRESCENT BOOKS

This edition published by:
Crescent Books
Distributed by Outlet Book Company
A Random House Company
225 Park Avenue South
New York, New York 10003

Printed and bound in U.S.A.

ISBN: 0-517-05895-2
Library of Congress Catalog Card Number: 91-61023

Pictured on the front cover: Charcoal Beef Kabobs *(page 9)* and Chili Tomato Grilled Chicken
(page 53).

Pictured on the back cover, clockwise from top left: Western Lamb Riblets *(page 28)*, Salmon
Steaks in Orange-Honey Marinade *(page 54)*, Ice Cream Cookie Sandwiches *(page 83)* and
Ranch Picnic Potato Salad *(page 66)*.

8   7   6   5   4   3   2

Contents

Barbecue Basics

CHOOSING A GRILL

Before you purchase a grill, consider where you grill, what you'll be cooking, the seasons you'll be grilling and the size of your budget. A small portable grill is fine if you usually barbecue smaller cuts of meat for a few people. For larger cuts of meat, bigger groups of people and year-round grilling, a large covered grill is worth the expense. Basic types of grills include: gas, brazier, covered cooker, water smoker and portable.

Gas Grill: Fast starts, accurate heat control, even cooking and year-round use make this the most convenient type of grill. Bottled gas is fed into burners under a bed of lava rock or ceramic coals—no charcoal is required.

Brazier: Simple models have hollowed fire bowls set on three or four legs. More elaborate braziers have half-hoods, covers, rotisseries and wheels.

Covered Cooker: Square, rectangular or kettle-shaped, this versatile grill does everything a brazier does. The cover also lets you roast, steam, smoke or cook whole meals in any season of the year. Draft controls on the lid and the base help control temperature.

Water Smoker: This is a heavy, dome-covered grill with two pans—one for charcoal and, above it, one for water. When the grill is covered, steam slowly cooks the food. Hickory chips or other aromatic wood can be added. The water smoker doubles as an open brazier when you remove the water pan and place the charcoal pan directly under the food.

Portable Grills: These include the familiar hibachi and small picnic grills on collapsible legs.

BARBECUE TOOLS AND ACCESSORIES

These tools will help make your barbecue cooking safer and more convenient.

Long-Handled Tongs, Basting Brush and Spatula: Moving hot coals and food around the grill, as well as basting and turning foods, can be dangerous. Select tools with long handles and hang them where you are working. You may want to purchase two pairs of tongs, one for coals and one for food.

Meat Thermometer: There is no better way to judge the doneness of meat than with a good quality meat thermometer that has been kept clean and in working order. Always remember to insert the thermometer into the center of the largest muscle of the meat, with the point away from bone, fat and rotisserie rod.

Heavy-Duty Mitts: You will prevent many burns by safeguarding your hands with big, thick mitts. Keep them close to the barbecue so they are always there when you need them.

Aluminum Foil Drip Pans: A drip pan placed beneath grilling meats will prevent flare-ups. The pan should be 1½ inches deep and extend about 3 inches beyond either end of the meat. The juices that collect in the drip pan may be used for a sauce or gravy.

Water Spritzer: For safety's sake, it's a good idea to keep a water-filled spray bottle near the barbecue for dousing flare-ups.

Other Tools and Accessories: A charcoal chimney or electric charcoal starter is useful for starting the fire without lighter fluid. Hinged wire baskets facilitate the turning of some foods, such as fish fillets. Long skewers made of noncorrosive metal or bamboo are indispensable for kabobs. Bamboo skewers should be soaked in water at least 20 minutes before grilling to prevent the bamboo from flaring up.

HOW TO LIGHT A CHARCOAL FIRE

The number of coals needed to barbecue foods depends on the size and type of grill and type and amount of food to be cooked. Certain weather conditions, such as wind, cold and high humidity, will require more coals to be used.

Arrange coals in a pyramid shape in center of grill 20 to 30 minutes before cooking. To start with lighter fluid, soak coals with about ½ cup of lighter fluid. Wait 1 minute, then light with a match.

To start with an electric starter, place starter in center of coals. Plug in 8 to 10 minutes or until ash begins to form around edges of coals. Unplug starter and remove. The electric starter will be very hot and should be placed in a safe, heat-resistant place to cool.

To start with a chimney starter, remove grid from grill and place chimney starter in the base of the grill. Crumble a few sheets of newspaper and place in bottom of chimney starter. Place coals on top of newspaper, then light the newspaper. The coals will be ready for grilling in 20 to 30 minutes. Carefully remove chimney starter. Be sure to wear mitts. This method does not use starter fluid.

When coals are ready, they will be ash gray during daylight and will glow at night. Spread coals into a single layer with tongs. To lower cooking temperature, spread coals farther apart or raise the grid, if possible. To make fire hotter, move coals closer together and tap off ash.

ARRANGING COALS FOR COOKING

For **direct cooking,** arrange the coals in a single layer directly under the food. Use this method for quick-cooking foods, such as hamburgers, steaks and fish.

For **indirect cooking,** arrange coals to one side of the grill. Place a drip pan under the food at the other side. For more heat, divide the coals on either side of the drip pan. Use this method for slow-cooking foods, such as roasts and whole chicken.

CHECKING CHARCOAL TEMPERATURE

To check the temperature of the coals, cautiously hold the palm of your hand about 4 inches above the coals. Count the number of seconds you can hold your hand in that position before the heat forces you to pull it away.

Seconds	Coal Temperature
2	hot, 375°F or more
3	medium-hot, 350°F to 375°F
4	medium, 300°F to 350°F
5	low, 200°F to 300°F

MARINATING TIPS

• Marinades add unique flavors to foods and help tenderize less-tender cuts of meat. Turn marinating foods occasionally to let the flavor infuse evenly.

Heavy-duty plastic bags are great to hold foods as they marinate.

• After food is removed from a marinade, the marinade may be used as a basting or dipping sauce. When using as a basting sauce, allow food to cook on the grill at least 5 minutes after the last application of marinade. When using as a dipping sauce, place marinade in a small saucepan and bring to a full boil. These precautions are necessary to prevent the cooked food from becoming contaminated with bacteria now present in the marinade from the raw food.

• Basting sauces containing sugar, honey or tomato products should be applied only during the last 15 to 30 minutes of grilling. This will prevent the food from charring. Basting sauces made from seasoned oils and butters may be brushed on throughout grilling.

BARBECUE TIPS

• Cleanup is easier if the grill rack is coated with vegetable oil or vegetable oil cooking spray before grilling.

• For barbecue safety, position the grill on a heat-proof surface, away from trees and bushes that could catch a spark and out of the path of traffic. Also, make sure the grill's vents are not clogged with ashes before starting a fire.

• To avoid flare-ups and charred food when grilling, remove visible fat from meat.

• If you partially cook foods in the microwave or on the range, immediately finish cooking the food on the grill. Do not refrigerate partially cooked foods or let them sit at room temperature before you complete cooking on the grill.

• Always serve cooked food from the grill on a clean plate, not one that held the raw food.

• In hot weather, food should never sit out for over 1 hour. Remember, keep hot foods hot and cold foods cold.

• For the best kabobs, parboil solid or starchy vegetables, such as carrots or potatoes, before using.

• Use long-handled tongs or spatula to turn meat. A fork or knife punctures meat and lets the juices escape.

• Use a meat thermometer to accurately determine the doneness of large cuts of meat or poultry cooked on the rotisserie or covered grill.

• For additional flavor, toss water-soaked wood chips, such as hickory or mesquite, onto hot coals before adding food. Adding wood chips to the coals will create smoke, so make sure the grill is in a well-ventilated area away from any open windows.

• Watch foods carefully during grilling. Total cooking time will vary with the type of food, position on the grill, weather, temperature of the coals and degree of doneness you desire.

• If you plan on grilling for more than 45 minutes, add 10 to 12 new coals around edges of coals just before you begin to cook. When the new coals are ready, move them to the center of the fire.

For the Barbecue Novice

These easy-to-prepare, easy-to-grill recipes will make your guests and family think you're an experienced barbecue chef!

SCANDINAVIAN BURGERS

  1 pound lean ground beef
  ¾ cup shredded zucchini
  ⅓ cup shredded carrot
  2 tablespoons finely minced onion
  1 tablespoon fresh chopped dill *or*
    1 teaspoon dried dill weed
  ½ teaspoon salt
    Dash freshly ground pepper
  1 egg, beaten
  ¼ cup beer
  4 whole-wheat buns or rye rolls (optional)

Preheat grill. Combine ground beef, zucchini, carrot, onion and seasonings in medium bowl; mix lightly. Stir in egg and beer. Shape into four patties.

Grill 8 minutes or to desired doneness, turning once. Serve on whole-wheat buns or rye rolls, if desired. *Makes 4 servings*

GRILLED SMOKED SAUSAGE

  1 cup apricot or pineapple preserves
  1 tablespoon lemon juice
  1½ pounds smoked sausage

Heat preserves and strain; reserve fruit pieces. Combine strained preserve liquid with lemon juice. Grill whole sausage, on uncovered grill, over low KINGSFORD® Briquets 5 minutes. Brush with glaze; continue to grill and glaze sausage about 5 minutes longer, turning occasionally. Garnish with fruit pieces.
Makes 6 servings

Top to bottom: Scandinavian Burgers, Grilled Smoked Sausage

BARBECUED ALASKA SALMON

2 whole Alaska salmon fillets (about
   1½ pounds each)
  Salt and pepper
½ cup butter or margarine, melted
¼ cup fresh lemon juice
4 teaspoons grated onion
1 teaspoon grated lemon peel
½ teaspoon hot pepper sauce

Rinse salmon fillets with cold water; pat dry
with paper toweling. Sprinkle both sides of
each fillet with salt and pepper. Combine
remaining ingredients; brush both sides of
fillets with butter mixture. Place each fillet,
skin side down, on sheet of well-oiled heavy-
duty foil. Grill salmon on uncovered grill over
hot coals 10 minutes per inch of thickness
measured at its thickest part, or until salmon
flakes easily when tested with fork. Baste often
with butter mixture.

Makes 12 to 16 servings

*Favorite Recipe from **Alaska Seafood Marketing Institute***

Barbecued Alaska Salmon

GRILLED MEXICAN-STYLE BURGERS

1 pound ground beef
2 teaspoons instant minced onion
¾ teaspoon *each* dried oregano leaves,
   ground cumin and salt
¼ teaspoon pepper
1 small tomato, cut into 8 thin slices
4 taco shells or flour tortillas
1 cup shredded lettuce
¼ cup salsa

Combine ground beef, onion, oregano, cumin,
salt and pepper, mixing lightly but thoroughly.
Divide beef mixture into 4 equal portions;
form each into an oval-shaped patty
(6×2½ inches). Grill patties on grid over
medium coals, turning once. Grill 10 minutes
for rare; 12 minutes for medium. To assemble,
arrange 2 tomato slices and a grilled burger in
each taco shell. Top each with ¼ cup lettuce
and 1 tablespoon salsa. *Makes 4 servings*

*Favorite Recipe from **National Live Stock and Meat Board***

SOUTHWESTERN FRANKFURTERS

1 pound beef frankfurters (8 to 10)
½ cup chopped cucumber
1 medium tomato, chopped
1 can (4 ounces) chopped green chilies,
   undrained
½ teaspoon ground cumin
8 to 10 taco shells
½ avocado, peeled, seeded and cut into
   8 to 10 slices

Place frankfurters on grid over medium coals.
Grill 8 to 10 minutes, turning occasionally.
Meanwhile, combine cucumber, tomato, chilies
and cumin. Place 1 tablespoon cucumber
relish in each taco shell; top with grilled
frankfurter. Place avocado slice on one side of
each frankfurter; top with an additional
tablespoon of relish.

Makes 8 to 10 servings

*Favorite Recipe from **National Live Stock and Meat Board***

Charcoal Beef Kabobs

CHARCOAL BEEF KABOBS

½ cup vegetable oil
¼ cup lemon juice
1½ tablespoons (½ package) HIDDEN
     VALLEY RANCH® Salad Dressing Mix
2 pounds beef top round or boneless
     sirloin steak, cut into 1-inch cubes
1 or 2 red, yellow or green peppers, cut
     into 1-inch squares
16 pearl onions *or* 1 medium onion, cut
     into wedges
8 cherry tomatoes

Combine oil, lemon juice and dry salad
dressing mix. Pour over beef cubes in shallow
dish. Cover and refrigerate 1 hour or longer.
Drain beef; reserve marinade. Thread beef
cubes, peppers and onion onto skewers. Grill
kabobs, on uncovered grill, over medium-hot
KINGSFORD® Briquets 15 minutes, brushing
often with reserved marinade and turning to
brown all sides. A few minutes before serving,
add cherry tomatoes to ends of skewers.

Makes 4 servings

Ranch Burgers

RANCH BURGERS

1¼ pounds lean ground beef
¾ cup prepared HIDDEN VALLEY
    RANCH® Original Ranch® Salad
    Dressing
¾ cup dry bread crumbs
¼ cup minced onion
1 teaspoon salt
¼ teaspoon black pepper
   Sesame seed buns
   Lettuce, tomato slices and red onion
    slices (optional)
   HIDDEN VALLEY RANCH® Original
    Ranch® Salad Dressing

In large bowl, combine beef, ¾ cup salad dressing, bread crumbs, onion, salt and pepper. Shape into 6 patties. Grill over medium-hot coals 4 to 5 minutes for medium doneness. Place on sesame seed buns with lettuce, tomatoes and red onions, if desired. Serve with a generous amount of additional salad dressing. *Makes 6 servings*

PACIFIC COAST BARBECUED SALMON

4 fresh or frozen salmon steaks, 1 inch
   thick (about 8 ounces each)
½ cup butter or margarine
2 tablespoons fresh lemon juice
1 tablespoon Worcestershire sauce

Thaw salmon steaks, if frozen. In saucepan,
combine butter, lemon juice and
Worcestershire sauce; simmer 5 minutes,
stirring frequently. Brush salmon steaks with
butter mixture. Place steaks in well-greased
wire grill basket.

Grill steaks, on uncovered grill, over medium-
hot KINGSFORD® Briquets 6 to 9 minutes or
until lightly browned. Baste steaks with butter
mixture and turn; grill 6 to 9 minutes longer,
basting often, until fish flakes easily when
tested with fork.   *Makes 4 servings*

SALSA-MARINATED CHUCK STEAK

1 pound boneless beef chuck shoulder
   steak, cut 1 inch thick
½ cup medium salsa
⅓ cup fresh lime juice
2 tablespoons hoisin sauce*
2 teaspoons grated fresh ginger

Combine salsa, lime juice, hoisin sauce and
ginger. Place beef chuck shoulder steak in
plastic bag; add ½ salsa mixture, turning to
coat steak. Close bag securely; marinate in
refrigerator 6 to 8 hours (or overnight, if
desired), turning at least once. Remove steak
from marinade; discard marinade. Place steak
on grid over medium coals. Grill to desired
doneness (rare to medium), 14 to 20 minutes,
turning once and brushing occasionally with
reserved ½ salsa mixture. Carve steak into
thin slices.   *Makes 4 servings*

*Hoisin sauce is available in the Oriental
section of the supermarket.

*Favorite Recipe from **National Live Stock and Meat Board***

Pacific Coast Barbecued Salmon

GRILLED RAINBOW TROUT WITH ITALIAN BUTTER

2 tablespoons butter or margarine, softened
1 tablespoon finely chopped red bell pepper
½ teaspoon dried Italian seasonings
4 CLEAR SPRINGS® Brand Idaho Rainbow Trout fillets (4 ounces each)
2 tablespoons grated Parmesan cheese (optional)

Cream butter, pepper and seasonings; chill and set aside. Over hot coals, place trout fillets, flesh side down, on oiled grid and cook about 2 minutes. Gently turn trout with spatula; continue cooking 2 minutes longer. Serve immediately with a dollop of Italian Butter and a sprinkle of Parmesan cheese.

Makes 4 servings

ISLANDER'S BEEF BARBECUE

3- to 3½-pound boneless beef chuck roast
¾ cup apricot-pineapple jam
2 tablespoons soy sauce
1 teaspoon ground ginger
1 teaspoon grated lemon peel

Slice roast across grain into ¼-inch-thick slices. Combine remaining ingredients in bowl; mix well. Grill beef slices, on uncovered grill, over medium-hot KINGSFORD® Briquets 8 to 10 minutes. Turn and baste often with jam mixture. *Makes 4 to 6 servings*

Note: If time permits, pierce meat several times with fork and marinate in jam mixture 1 to 4 hours in refrigerator. Drain meat; reserve jam mixture. Continue as directed above.

BEEF KABOBS ITALIANO

1 (8-ounce) can tomato sauce
⅓ cup REALEMON® Lemon Juice from Concentrate
2 tablespoons brown sugar
2 teaspoons WYLER'S® or STEERO® Beef-Flavor Instant Bouillon
1½ teaspoons thyme leaves
1 pound beef sirloin steak (about 1½ inch thick), cut into cubes
1 large green bell pepper, cut into bite-size pieces
2 medium onions, quartered and separated into bite-size pieces
8 ounces medium fresh mushrooms (about 2 cups)
½ pint cherry tomatoes

In shallow dish or plastic bag, combine tomato sauce, ReaLemon® brand, sugar, bouillon and thyme; mix well. Add meat. Cover; marinate in refrigerator 6 hours or overnight. Skewer meat with vegetables. Grill or broil as desired, basting frequently with marinade. Refrigerate leftovers. *Makes 4 servings*

CHICKEN ITALIANO

½ cup WISH-BONE® Italian Dressing or Herbal Italian Dressing
2½ to 3 pounds chicken pieces*

In large shallow baking dish, pour Italian dressing over chicken. Cover and marinate in refrigerator, turning occasionally, 4 hours or overnight. Remove chicken; reserve marinade.

Grill or broil chicken, turning and basting frequently with reserved marinade, until done.
Makes about 4 servings

*Use 1 (2½- to 3-pound) beef London broil or beef round steak for chicken pieces.

ALL-AMERICAN CHEESEBURGERS

1 pound lean ground beef
1 tablespoon WYLER'S® or STEERO®
   Beef-Flavor Instant Bouillon
¼ cup chopped onion
4 slices BORDEN® Process American
   Cheese Food
4 hamburger buns, split, buttered and
   toasted
   Lettuce
4 slices tomato

In medium bowl, combine beef, bouillon and onion; mix well. Shape into 4 patties. Grill or broil to desired doneness. Top with cheese food slices; heat until cheese food begins to melt. Top bottom halves of buns with lettuce, tomato and meat patties. Serve open-face or with bun tops. Refrigerate leftovers.

Makes 4 servings

VARIATIONS

Santa Fe Burgers: Add 3 tablespoons salsa or taco sauce to ground beef. On warm tortilla, spread refried beans; top with shredded lettuce, cooked burger, cheese food slice, salsa and sour cream.

Kansas City Burgers: Add ½ cup thawed frozen hash browns and 2 tablespoons barbecue sauce to ground beef. Place each cooked burger on bun; top with cheese food slice, cooked, crumbled bacon and sliced green onion.

Manhattan Burgers: Add ¼ cup pizza sauce, 2 tablespoons chopped mushrooms and 3 tablespoons chopped pepperoni to ground beef. Place each cooked burger on grilled Italian bread; top with cheese food slice, pepperoni and green pepper.

Clockwise from left: Santa Fe Burger, Kansas City Burger, Manhattan Burger

Parmesan Seasoned Turkey

PARMESAN SEASONED TURKEY

  2 tablespoons butter or margarine, melted
1½ teaspoons grated Parmesan cheese
     Dash coarsely ground black pepper
     Dash crushed red pepper
     Dash onion powder
  4 slices BUTTERBALL® Slice 'N Serve
     Breast of Turkey, cut ⅜ inch thick

Combine butter, cheese, peppers and onion powder in small dish. Brush both sides of turkey with seasoned butter. Grill over medium coals 6 to 8 minutes or until hot. Turn over halfway through heating.

Makes 4 servings

GRILLED HAKE FILLETS

  2 pounds hake fillets, fresh or frozen
¼ cup French dressing
  1 tablespoon lemon juice
  1 tablespoon grated onion
  2 teaspoons salt
     Dash pepper

Thaw fish, if frozen. Cut into serving-size portions. Mix remaining ingredients in small bowl until blended. Baste fish with sauce. Arrange fish on well-greased grid. Grill, 4 inches from moderately hot coals, 15 to 18 minutes or until fish flakes easily when tested with fork. Turn and baste with remaining sauce halfway through cooking.

Makes 6 servings

*Favorite Recipe from **National Fisheries Institute***

Sizzling Meats

Try your hand with these saucy ribs, tasty burgers, eye-catching kabobs and succulent steaks grilled to flavorful perfection.

HOT AND SPICY SPARERIBS

   1 rack pork spareribs, 3 pounds
   2 tablespoons butter or margarine
   1 medium onion, finely chopped
   2 cloves garlic, minced
   1 can (15 ounces) tomato sauce
   ⅔ cup cider vinegar
   ⅔ cup firmly packed brown sugar
   2 tablespoons chili powder
   1 tablespoon prepared mustard
   ½ teaspoon pepper

Melt butter in large skillet over low heat; add onion and garlic and sauté until tender. Add remaining ingredients, except ribs, and bring to a boil. Reduce heat and simmer 20 minutes, stirring occasionally.

Place large piece of aluminum foil over coals beneath grill to catch drippings. Baste meatiest side of ribs with sauce. Place ribs on grill, meatiest side down, about 6 inches above low coals; baste top side. Close grill hood. Cook about 20 minutes; turn ribs and baste. Cook 45 minutes more or until done, basting every 10 to 15 minutes with sauce.

Makes 3 servings

Favorite Recipe from **National Pork Producers Council**

ORIENTAL STEAK KABOBS

   1 cup (8 ounces) WISH-BONE® Italian, Robusto Italian or Lite Italian Dressing
   ¼ cup soy sauce
   2 tablespoons brown sugar
   ½ teaspoon ground ginger
   1 green onion, thinly sliced
   1 pound boneless beef round, cut into 1-inch pieces
  12 large mushrooms
   2 cups broccoli florets
   1 medium red pepper, cut into chunks

In large shallow baking dish, combine Italian dressing, soy sauce, brown sugar, ginger and onion. Add beef and vegetables; turn to coat. Cover and marinate in refrigerator, stirring occasionally, 4 hours or overnight. Remove beef and vegetables; reserve marinade.

Onto large skewers, thread beef with vegetables. Grill or broil, turning and basting frequently with reserved marinade, 10 minutes or until beef is done.

Makes about 4 servings

Hot and Spicy Spareribs

HONEY-GARLIC AMERICA'S CUT

    4 America's Cut boneless center pork loin
        chops, 1¼ to 1½ inches thick
    ¼ cup lemon juice
    ¼ cup honey
    2 tablespoons soy sauce
    1 tablespoon dry sherry
    2 cloves garlic, minced

Place chops in heavy plastic bag. Combine remaining ingredients in small bowl. Pour over chops, turning bag to coat. Close bag; refrigerate 4 to 24 hours.

Prepare covered grill with drip pan in center banked by medium-hot coals. Remove chops from marinade; reserve marinade. Grill chops 12 to 15 minutes, turning once and basting occasionally with reserved marinade.

Makes 4 servings

*Favorite Recipe from **National Pork Producers Council***

SPICY LAMB BURGERS

    ¼ cup chopped onion
    1 teaspoon curry powder
    1 tablespoon butter or margarine, melted
    ¼ cup finely chopped almonds
    ¼ cup crushed pineapple, drained
    1½ pounds ground lamb
    ½ cup dry bread crumbs
    2 eggs
    ⅛ teaspoon pepper
    6 pita breads

Cook onion and curry powder in butter until onion is tender. Stir in almonds and crushed pineapple. Mix thoroughly with lamb, bread crumbs, eggs and pepper. Shape meat mixture into 6 patties. Grill patties, on uncovered grill, over medium-hot MATCH LIGHT® Charcoal Briquets about 5 minutes on each side, or until done. Grill pita breads on edge of grill. Serve lamb burgers in pita breads.

Makes 6 servings

Honey-Garlic America's Cut

Greek Burgers

GREEK BURGERS

Yogurt Sauce (recipe follows)
1 pound ground beef
2 tablespoons red wine
2 teaspoons ground cumin
1 tablespoon chopped fresh oregano *or*
    1 teaspoon dried oregano leaves
½ teaspoon salt
    Dash ground red pepper
    Dash ground black pepper
4 pita breads
    Lettuce
    Chopped tomatoes

Prepare Yogurt Sauce. Soak 4 bamboo skewers in water at least 20 minutes before using. Combine meat, wine and seasonings in medium bowl; mix lightly. Divide mixture into eight equal portions; form each portion into an oval, each about 4 inches long. Cover; chill 30 minutes.

Preheat grill. Insert skewers lengthwise through centers of ovals, placing 2 on each skewer. Grill about 8 minutes or to desired doneness, turning once. Fill pita breads with lettuce, meat and chopped tomatoes. Serve with Yogurt Sauce. *Makes 4 servings*

YOGURT SAUCE

2 cups plain yogurt
1 cup chopped red onion
1 cup chopped cucumber
¼ cup chopped fresh mint *or*
    1½ tablespoons dried mint leaves
1 tablespoon chopped fresh marjoram or
    1 teaspoon dried marjoram leaves

Combine ingredients in small bowl. Cover; chill up to 4 hours before serving.

Apricot-Glazed Lamb Chops

GRILLED SAUSAGE WITH SWEET POTATO AND APPLE KABOBS

1 pound fresh country-style pork sausage
    links, bratwurst or Polish sausage
¼ cup apple jelly, melted
½ teaspoon orange or lemon juice
    Dash allspice
    Dash nutmeg
1 large sweet potato, cut crosswise into
    ¾-inch slices (about 12 ounces)
1 large apple, cored, cut into 8 wedges
1 tablespoon butter or margarine, melted

Combine jelly, orange juice, allspice and nutmeg. Parboil sweet potatoes in boiling water 7 minutes; drain. Thread sweet potato slices and apple wedges on four 12-inch skewers. Brush lightly with butter. Place sausages on grid over low to medium coals. Grill 5 minutes. Place kabobs on grid and brush sausage and kabobs with apple jelly mixture. Grill 10 minutes, turning and brushing with jelly mixture after 5 minutes. Internal temperature of sausage should register 170°F. *Makes 4 servings*

*Favorite Recipe from **National Live Stock and Meat Board***

APRICOT-GLAZED LAMB CHOPS

⅓ cup apricot jam
1 tablespoon white vinegar
1 teaspoon Dijon-style mustard
½ teaspoon dried rosemary leaves
½ teaspoon salt
1 clove garlic, minced
¼ teaspoon pepper
4 lamb shoulder or blade chops, cut
    ¾ inch thick

Combine apricot jam, vinegar, mustard, rosemary, salt, garlic and pepper in small saucepan; cook slowly, stirring, until melted. Grill lamb chops, on uncovered grill, over medium coals 14 to 16 minutes for medium, turning once. Brush both sides with glaze several times during grilling.

Makes 4 to 5 servings

*Favorite Recipe from **National Live Stock and Meat Board***

Grilled Sausage with Sweet Potato and Apple Kabobs

Fajitas

FAJITAS

Pico de Gallo Sauce (recipe follows)
2 pounds boneless beef skirt steak or flank
   steak
¾ cup beer
½ cup lime juice
2 tablespoons Worcestershire sauce
8 (6-inch) flour tortillas

Prepare Pico de Gallo Sauce. Trim excess fat
from steak; place in shallow glass dish.
Combine beer, lime juice and Worcestershire
sauce; pour over steak. Cover and refrigerate
overnight, spooning marinade over meat
occasionally.

Drain steak; reserve marinade. Pat steak dry
with paper toweling. Grill steak, on covered
grill, over medium-hot KINGSFORD® Briquets
8 to 10 minutes, basting meat occasionally
with reserved marinade. Turn and grill to
desired doneness, allowing 8 to 10 minutes
longer for medium. Carve meat across grain
into thin slices.

Meanwhile, wrap tortillas in heavy-duty foil;
place tortillas at edge of grill 5 minutes or until
heated through. Wrap steak slices in warmed
tortillas; top with chilled Pico de Gallo Sauce.
Makes 8 servings

PICO DE GALLO SAUCE

3 medium tomatoes, peeled and chopped
½ cup chopped green onions
1 large Anaheim chili pepper, chopped
1 fresh jalapeño chili pepper, seeded and
   chopped
2 teaspoons chopped fresh cilantro or
   parsley
1 teaspoon salt

In small bowl, combine tomatoes, onions,
peppers, cilantro and salt. Cover and
refrigerate 5 hours or overnight.
Makes about 1¾ cups

Flank Steak Teriyaki with Savory Rice

FLANK STEAK TERIYAKI WITH SAVORY RICE

½ cup peanut or vegetable oil
¼ cup dry red wine
3 tablespoons teriyaki sauce
1 jar (12 ounces) roasted red peppers, drained and chopped
2 tablespoons light brown sugar
1 tablespoon plus 1 teaspoon finely chopped garlic
⅛ teaspoon crushed red pepper
½ pound beef flank steak, sliced diagonally into ¼-inch strips
2 tablespoons butter or margarine
1 teaspoon finely chopped fresh ginger (optional)
½ cup thinly sliced zucchini
2 cups water
1 package LIPTON® Rice & Sauce – Herb & Butter
Pepper to taste

In large shallow glass baking dish, thoroughly combine oil, wine, teriyaki sauce, 1 cup roasted peppers, brown sugar, 1 tablespoon garlic and crushed red pepper. Add steak and turn to coat. Cover and marinate in refrigerator, turning occasionally, at least 4 hours. Remove steak, reserving marinade.

Onto 4 large skewers, thread steak, weaving back and forth. Grill or broil, turning and basting with reserved marinade, 3 minutes or until done.

Meanwhile, in large skillet, melt butter and cook remaining 1 teaspoon garlic with ginger over medium-high heat 30 seconds. Add zucchini and cook, stirring frequently, 2 minutes or until tender. Stir in water and rice & herb & butter sauce and bring to a boil. Reduce heat and simmer, stirring occasionally, 10 minutes or until rice is tender. Stir in remaining roasted peppers and pepper. Serve rice with steak. *Makes about 2 servings*

BLUE CHEESE BURGERS

1¼ pounds lean ground beef
  1 tablespoon finely chopped onion
1½ teaspoons chopped fresh thyme *or*
      ½ teaspoon dried thyme leaves
  ¾ teaspoon salt
      Dash ground pepper
  4 ounces blue cheese, crumbled
      Lettuce, tomato slices, Dijon-style
         mustard (optional)
  4 whole-wheat buns, split (optional)

Preheat grill. Combine ground beef, onion and seasonings in medium bowl; mix lightly. Shape into eight patties.

Place cheese in center of four patties to within ½ inch of outer edge; top with remaining burgers. Press edges together to seal.

Grill 8 minutes or to desired doneness, turning once. Serve with lettuce, tomatoes and Dijon-style mustard on whole-wheat buns, if desired.

Makes 4 servings

STEAK PORT ANTONIO

  ¼ cup rum
  1 tablespoon chopped shallots
  4 tablespoons butter or margarine
  1 tablespoon chopped parsley
  2 teaspoons lime juice
  ½ teaspoon TABASCO® Pepper Sauce
  4 beef shell steaks

In saucepan, combine rum and shallots; bring to a boil. Reduce heat; simmer 2 minutes. Stir in butter, parsley, lime juice and Tabasco® sauce.

Brush steaks with rum butter. Grill or broil 6 inches from heat. Cook about 8 minutes, turning steak once. Brush occasionally with rum butter. Heat any remaining rum butter to a boil and serve with steaks. Serve with additional Tabasco® sauce.

Makes 4 servings

BARBECUED PORK CHOPS

  6 pork loin chops, cut 1 inch thick
  ½ teaspoon seasoned salt
  6 slices orange
  6 thin slices onion
  6 thin slices lemon
  ⅓ cup K.C. MASTERPIECE® Barbecue
      Sauce

Arrange medium-hot KINGSFORD® Briquets to one side of grill with drip pan next to briquets. Sprinkle chops with seasoned salt. Place chops over drip pan; cover grill and cook 40 minutes or until nearly done, turning once after 25 minutes.

Top each chop with slices of orange, onion, lemon and about 1 tablespoon barbecue sauce. Cover grill and cook 5 to 10 minutes longer or until chops are tender and thoroughly cooked.

Makes 6 servings

Barbecued Pork Chops

GRILLED LAMB FAJITAS

 3 tablespoons olive oil
 3 tablespoons tequila or orange juice
 2 tablespoons fresh lime juice
 1 teaspoon ground cumin
 1 teaspoon chili powder
 1 teaspoon dried oregano leaves, crushed
 ½ teaspoon salt
 ¼ teaspoon black pepper
 ¼ teaspoon red pepper flakes, crushed
 ¼ cup chopped fresh cilantro
 1½ pounds lean American lamb leg steaks,
      cut 1 inch thick
 6 green onions
 3 fresh poblano or ancho chilies (optional)
 1 red pepper, halved and seeded
 1 green pepper, halved and seeded
 1 yellow pepper, halved and seeded
 12 medium flour tortillas, warmed
      Salsa

For marinade, in small bowl combine oil, tequila, lime juice, cumin, chili powder, oregano, salt, black pepper, red pepper flakes and cilantro. Place lamb in glass dish. Pour marinade over lamb; cover and refrigerate 4 to 6 hours.

Ignite coals in barbecue; allow to burn until bright red and covered with gray ash. Drain lamb; discard marinade. Grill lamb, onions, chilies and red, green and yellow peppers 4 inches from coals. Cook steaks 5 to 6 minutes per side for medium-rare or to desired degree of doneness. Turn vegetables frequently until cooked. Slice lamb steaks and vegetables into ¼-inch-thick slices. Serve on tortillas, top with salsa and roll up.

Makes 12 servings

*Favorite Recipe from **American Lamb Council***

Grilled Lamb Fajitas

Barbecued Beef Short Ribs

BARBECUED BEEF SHORT RIBS

6 pounds beef chuck ribs, cut into 1-rib pieces
1 cup water
¾ cup soy sauce
⅔ cup dry sherry
½ cup packed dark brown sugar
6 cloves garlic, minced
1 tablespoon ground red pepper
1 tablespoon grated fresh ginger
2 teaspoons Chinese five spice powder

Trim excess fat from ribs. In large roasting pan, arrange ribs in single layer. For marinade, in medium saucepan combine remaining ingredients. Cook over medium heat on range top until sugar is dissolved. Remove from heat; cool slightly. Pour marinade over ribs. Cover and marinate in refrigerator 1 hour, turning ribs once.

Cover roasting pan with foil. Arrange medium-hot KINGSFORD® Briquets around drip pan. Place roasting pan on grid; cover grill and cook ribs 45 minutes. Remove ribs from roasting pan and place directly on grid; reserve marinade. Continue cooking, in covered grill, 45 to 60 minutes longer or until ribs are tender, turning occasionally. Brush ribs again with reserved marinade just before serving.

Makes 8 servings

BUTTERFLIED LEG OF LAMB WITH ORANGE SAUCE

3½- to 4-pound butterflied lamb leg
⅔ cup orange juice
½ cup orange marmalade
1 teaspoon butter or margarine
½ teaspoon grated fresh ginger
¼ teaspoon dry mustard
2 tablespoons lemon juice
1 tablespoon cornstarch

Thread 2 long metal skewers through butterflied lamb leg to secure and facilitate turning the roast. Grill lamb, on covered grill, over medium coals to desired doneness. Allow 40 to 60 minutes total cooking time.

Meanwhile, combine orange juice, marmalade, butter, ginger and mustard in small saucepan. Cook over medium-low heat until marmalade is melted, stirring occasionally. Combine lemon juice and cornstarch; stir into orange juice mixture and cook until thickened. Remove from heat; reserve. Turn leg several times during cooking, brushing with ⅓ cup reserved sauce during last 10 minutes of cooking. Remove skewers and separate leg into three sections along natural seams. Carve each section across grain into thin slices. Serve remaining sauce with carved lamb.

Makes 10 to 12 servings

*Favorite Recipe from **National Live Stock and Meat Board***

TEXAS BARBECUE BEEF BRISKET

  1 boneless beef brisket (6 to 8 pounds)
  2 teaspoons paprika
  1 teaspoon freshly ground black pepper, divided
  1 tablespoon butter or margarine
  1 medium onion, grated
1½ cups catsup
  1 tablespoon fresh lemon juice
  1 tablespoon Worcestershire sauce
  1 teaspoon hot pepper sauce

Trim external fat on beef brisket to ¼ inch. Combine paprika and ½ teaspoon of the black pepper; rub evenly over surface of beef brisket. Place brisket, fat side down, in 11½×9-inch disposable foil pan. Add 1 cup water. Cover pan tightly with aluminum foil. Place in center of grid over very low coals (use a single layer of coals with space in between each); cover cooker. Cook 5 hours, turning brisket over every 1½ hours; use baster to remove fat from pan as it accumulates. Add ½ cup water, if needed, to pan during cooking. (Add just enough briquets during cooking to keep coals at a very low temperature.) Remove brisket from pan; place on grid, fat side down, directly over very low coals. Reserve pan drippings. Cover; continue cooking 30 minutes.

Meanwhile, skim fat from pan drippings; reserve 1 cup drippings. Melt butter in medium saucepan over medium heat. Add onion; cook until tender-crisp. Add reserved pan drippings, remaining ½ teaspoon black pepper, the catsup, lemon juice, Worcestershire sauce and hot pepper sauce; simmer 15 minutes. Carve brisket into thin slices across grain; serve with sauce. Garnish with fresh peppers and lemon and lime slices.   *Makes 18 to 24 servings*

Note: For a smoky flavor, soak oak, pecan, mesquite or hickory chips in water 30 minutes and add to very low coals.

Favorite Recipe from **National Live Stock and Meat Board**

PEANUT PORK SATÉ

  1 cup (8 ounces) WISH-BONE® Sweet 'n Spicy French or Lite Sweet 'n Spicy French Dressing
  ¼ cup peanut butter
  1 tablespoon dry sherry
  2 teaspoons soy sauce
  ½ to 1 teaspoon crushed red pepper
  1 (1-inch) piece fresh ginger, peeled and cut into pieces *or* ½ teaspoon ground ginger
  1 medium clove garlic
  ¼ cup water
1½ pounds pork tenderloin, sliced diagonally into ¼-inch strips*

In blender or food processor, blend sweet 'n spicy French dressing, peanut butter, sherry, soy sauce, pepper, ginger and garlic until smooth.

In large shallow baking dish, blend ½ cup dressing mixture with water; add pork and turn to coat. Cover and marinate in refrigerator, stirring occasionally, 4 hours or overnight. Cover and refrigerate remaining dressing mixture for use as basting sauce. Remove pork from marinade; discard marinade.

Onto 12-inch skewers thread pork strips, weaving back and forth. Grill or broil, turning and basting occasionally with reserved dressing mixture, 12 minutes or until pork is done.   *Makes about 6 servings*

*Use 1½ pounds boneless beef flank or round steak, sliced diagonally into ¼-inch strips for the pork strips.

WESTERN LAMB RIBLETS

5 pounds lamb riblets, cut into serving-size pieces
¾ cup chili sauce
½ cup honey
½ cup beer
¼ cup Worcestershire sauce
¼ cup finely chopped onion
1 clove garlic, minced
½ teaspoon crushed red pepper

Trim excess fat from riblets. In saucepan, combine chili sauce, honey, beer, Worcestershire, onion, garlic and red pepper. On range top, heat mixture to boiling. Reduce heat; simmer, covered, 10 minutes. Remove from heat; cool.

Place riblets in plastic bag; pour marinade over riblets. Close bag; set bag in large bowl. Marinate riblets in refrigerator about 2 hours, turning bag occasionally to distribute marinade evenly.

Drain riblets; reserve marinade. Arrange medium-hot KINGSFORD® Briquets around drip pan. Place riblets over drip pan. Cover grill and cook 45 minutes, turning riblets and brushing with reserved marinade twice. Heat remaining marinade to boiling and serve with riblets. *Makes 6 servings*

CAROLINA PORK BARBECUE

4- to 5-pound boneless pork shoulder
(Boston Butt)
1 quart cider vinegar
1 to 1½ ounces crushed red pepper
1 tablespoon black pepper
Hush puppies (optional)
Coleslaw (optional)

Stir together vinegar and peppers. Prepare covered grill with drip pan in center banked by medium-hot coals. Place pork on grill over drip pan; close hood. Cook 2½ to 3½ hours until pork is very tender, basting frequently with vinegar marinade. Remove pork from grill; cool slightly. Chop meat and serve with hush puppies and cole slaw, if desired.

Makes about 12 servings

*Favorite Recipe from **National Pork Producers Council***

Western Lamb Riblets

Javanese Pork Saté and Raita (page 71)

JAVANESE PORK SATÉ

1 pound boneless pork loin
½ cup minced onion
2 tablespoons peanut butter
2 tablespoons lemon juice
2 tablespoons soy sauce
1 tablespoon brown sugar
1 tablespoon vegetable oil
1 clove garlic, minced
   Dash hot pepper sauce
   Raita (page 71)

Cut pork into ½-inch cubes; place in shallow dish. In blender or food processor combine remaining ingredients. Blend until smooth. Pour over pork. Cover and marinate in refrigerator 10 minutes. Thread pork on skewers (if using bamboo skewers, soak in water 1 hour to prevent burning).

Grill or broil 10 to 12 minutes, turning occasionally, until done. Serve with hot cooked rice, if desired. Serve with Raita.

Makes 4 servings

*Favorite Recipe from **National Pork Producers Council***

TEX-MEX FLANK STEAK

1 medium onion, thinly sliced
½ cup REALEMON® Lemon Juice from Concentrate
½ cup vegetable oil
2 tablespoons dry sherry
2 teaspoons WYLER'S® or STEERO® Beef-Flavor Instant Bouillon
2 teaspoons chili powder
2 teaspoons ground cumin
2 cloves garlic, finely chopped
1 (1- to 1½-pound) beef flank steak, scored

In shallow dish or plastic bag, combine all ingredients except meat; add meat. Cover; marinate in refrigerator 6 hours or overnight. Remove meat from marinade; grill or broil as desired, basting frequently with marinade.

Makes 4 to 6 servings

Grilled Steaks with Vegetables

1 inch thick require about 16 minutes for rare; 20 minutes for medium. Steaks cut 1½ inches thick require about 22 minutes for rare; 30 minutes for medium.) After turning steaks, heat oil in large heavy skillet on grid over coals. Add remaining clove garlic, the zucchini and onion; cook and stir 4 to 5 minutes. Add mushrooms, salt and remaining ¾ teaspoon basil; continue cooking 2 minutes, stirring frequently. Add tomatoes; heat through.

Makes 4 to 6 servings

*Favorite Recipe from **National Live Stock and Meat Board***

GRILLED STEAKS WITH VEGETABLES

2 beef Porterhouse steaks, cut 1 to
  1½ inches thick (about 1 pound each)
2 cloves garlic, finely minced, divided
1½ teaspoons dried basil leaves, divided
 ½ teaspoon coarse ground black pepper
1 tablespoon olive oil
1 large zucchini, cut into 2×½-inch pieces
1 small onion, cut into thin wedges
1¼ cups sliced fresh mushrooms
 ¼ teaspoon salt
6 cherry tomatoes, cut into halves

Season steaks with 1 clove of the garlic, ¾ teaspoon of the basil and the pepper. Place steaks on grid over medium coals. Grill to desired doneness, turning once. (Steaks cut

SNAPPY BEEF ROAST

1 boneless beef chuck eye roast or
  boneless chuck cross rib roast (3½ to
  4 pounds)
 ½ cup catsup
3 tablespoons fresh lemon juice
2 tablespoons vegetable oil
1½ tablespoons Worcestershire sauce
2 large cloves garlic, minced
1 teaspoon ground cumin
1 teaspoon salt
 ½ teaspoon ground red pepper

Combine catsup, lemon juice, vegetable oil, Worcestershire sauce, garlic, cumin, salt and red pepper. Brush mixture evenly over surface of beef chuck eye roast; place in large plastic bag. Close bag securely; refrigerate 12 hours (or overnight, if desired).

Insert meat thermometer in roast so bulb is centered in thickest part, not resting in fat. Cook in covered grill using indirect heat. Arrange coals on lower grid around outside edges; place drip pan between coals. When coals are ash-gray (about 30 minutes), place roast, fat side up, on grid above drip pan. Cover cooker, leaving all vents open. Cook roast to desired doneness, about 25 to 30 minutes per pound. Remove from grill when meat thermometer registers 135°F for rare or 155°F for medium. Allow roast to stand 15 to 20 minutes in warm place before carving. (Roast will continue to rise about 5°F in temperature to 140°F for rare and 160°F for medium.) Carve roast into thin slices.

Makes 12 to 16 servings

*Favorite Recipe from **National Live Stock and Meat Board***

LAMB SHASLEK
(Shish Kebab)

½ cup fresh lemon juice
3 tablespoons virgin olive oil
⅓ cup minced onion
4 cloves garlic, minced
1 tablespoon cracked pepper
1 teaspoon coarse salt
1½- pound fresh American lamb sirloin
      roast, cut into 2-inch cubes
1 small red onion, cut into 8 wedges
1 small white onion, cut into 8 wedges
1 lemon, cut into 8 wedges, for garnish

For marinade, in small bowl combine lemon juice, oil, minced onion, garlic, pepper and salt. In glass dish, place lamb and red and white onions. Pour marinade over lamb and onions; cover and refrigerate 6 to 24 hours. Stir lamb occasionally. Drain lamb and onions; discard marinade. Thread red onion, lamb and white onion onto skewers, ending with lemon wedge.

Ignite coals in barbecue; allow to burn until bright red and covered with gray ash. Grill lamb shaslek 4 inches from coals 5 to 6 minutes per side for medium-rare or until desired degree of doneness.

Makes 4 servings

*Favorite Recipe from **American Lamb Council***

Lamb Shaslek

Raspberry-Glazed Lamb Ribs

RASPBERRY-GLAZED LAMB RIBS

   2 Denver ribs of American lamb (about
     6 ounces), 8 ribs each
½ teaspoon salt
¼ teaspoon pepper
¼ teaspoon paprika
½ cup red wine vinegar or raspberry
   vinegar
½ cup white wine
½ cup raspberry jam, seedless
  1 tablespoon shallots, minced
  1 tablespoon cornstarch
  1 tablespoon water

One hour before grilling, rub salt, pepper and
paprika into lamb ribs. In medium saucepan,
combine vinegar, white wine, raspberry jam
and shallots. Stir over medium heat until jam is
melted. Stir together cornstarch and water; add
to raspberry mixture and stir sauce until
smooth and clear.

Preheat grill. Move hot white coals to each side
of grill. Place foil drip pan in center. Place
lamb ribs in center of pan. Cover and cook
50 to 60 minutes, turning every 10 minutes.
Brush on glaze during last 10 to 15 minutes of
grilling. *Makes 2 servings*

Favorite Recipe from American Lamb Council

TEXAS-STYLE STEAK ON HOT BREAD

½ cup olive or vegetable oil
¼ cup lime juice
¼ cup red wine vinegar
  1 medium onion, finely chopped
  1 large clove garlic, minced
  1 teaspoon chili powder
½ teaspoon salt
¼ teaspoon ground cumin
1½ pounds beef skirt or flank steak
  1 round loaf French or sourdough bread
  1 cup Mexican-style salsa
  1 cup guacamole

Combine oil, lime juice, vinegar, onion, garlic,
chili powder, salt and cumin in large glass dish.
Pound steak to ¼-inch thickness. Place steak in
marinade; turn to coat. Cover and refrigerate
overnight or several hours, turning several
times. Drain steak; discard marinade. Grill
steak, on covered grill, over medium-hot
KINGSFORD® with Mesquite Charcoal
Briquets 4 to 8 minutes on each side or until
done. Cut bread into 1-inch slices and toast on
grill. Heat salsa. Arrange steak, sliced into
¾-inch diagonal strips, on toasted bread. Top
with hot salsa and guacamole.
Makes 4 to 6 servings

CAMPERS' PIZZA

¼ pound ground beef (80% lean)
 1 medium onion, chopped
½ teaspoon salt
 1 can (8 ounces) refrigerated crescent rolls
 1 can (8 ounces) pizza sauce
 1 can (4 ounces) mushroom stems and pieces, drained and chopped
 1 can (2½ ounces) sliced pitted ripe olives, drained
⅓ cup coarsely chopped green bell pepper
 1 cup (4 ounces) shredded mozzarella cheese
 1 teaspoon dried oregano leaves

Brown ground beef and onion in well-seasoned 11- to 12-inch cast-iron skillet over medium coals. Remove to paper towels; season with salt. Pour off drippings from pan. Separate crescent dough into triangles; place in skillet, points toward center, to form circle. Press edges together to form bottom crust and 1-inch rim up side of pan. Spread half of pizza sauce over dough; spoon ground beef mixture over sauce. Top with mushrooms, olives and green pepper. Pour remaining sauce over all; sprinkle with cheese and oregano. Place pan in center of grid over medium coals. Place cover on grill; cook 20 to 30 minutes or until crust is lightly browned. *Makes 4 servings*

Note: If cooked over open grill or coals, cover pan securely with foil.

*Favorite Recipe from **National Live Stock and Meat Board***

Campers' Pizza

BARBECUED PORK LEG

1 fresh pork leg, skinned, boned, trimmed
   of fat, rolled and tied (14 to
   16 pounds)
Sam's Mop Sauce (recipe follows)
K.C. MASTERPIECE® Hickory
   Barbecue Sauce

Arrange medium-hot KINGSFORD® Briquets
around drip pan. Place prepared pork leg over
drip pan; cover grill and cook pork 4 to
4½ hours or until thermometer inserted into
thickest portion registers 170°F. Baste pork
with Sam's Mop Sauce every 30 minutes,
patting a thin coating of sauce on meat with
cotton swab mop or pastry brush. Let stand,
covered with foil, 10 minutes before serving.

Meanwhile, in saucepan, combine half the
remaining mop sauce with an equal amount of
barbecue sauce. Heat through and serve with
slices of pork.   *Makes about 20 servings*

Note: The final weight of the fresh pork leg for
grilling should be 8 to 10 pounds. To save time,
you can have the butcher prepare the fresh
pork leg for you.

SAM'S MOP SAUCE

   1 lemon
   1 cup water
   1 cup cider vinegar
   1 tablespoon butter or margarine
   1 tablespoon olive oil
   ½ teaspoon ground red pepper
1½ to 3 teaspoons hot pepper sauce
1½ to 3 teaspoons Worcestershire sauce
1½ teaspoons black pepper

With vegetable peeler, remove peel from
lemon; squeeze juice from lemon. In heavy
saucepan, combine lemon peel, juice and
remaining ingredients. Bring to boil. Place
saucepan on grill to keep warm, if space
permits.   *Makes 2¼ cups*

Barbecued Pork Leg

Beef Fajitas

BEEF FAJITAS

½ cup REALEMON® Lemon Juice from
    Concentrate
¼ cup vegetable oil
2 cloves garlic, finely chopped
2 teaspoons WYLER'S® or STEERO®
    Beef-Flavor Instant Bouillon
1 (1- to 1½-pound) beef top round steak
10 (6-inch) flour tortillas, warmed
    according to package directions
    Picante sauce, shredded lettuce,
    shredded cheddar cheese, sliced green
    onions for garnish

In shallow dish or plastic bag, combine
ReaLemon® brand, oil, garlic and bouillon; add
meat. Cover; marinate in refrigerator 6 hours
or overnight. Remove meat from marinade;
grill or broil as desired, basting frequently with
marinade. Slice meat diagonally into thin
strips; place on tortillas. Top with one or more
garnishes; fold tortillas. Serve immediately.
Refrigerate leftovers. *Makes 10 fajitas*

HONEY MUSTARD PORK TENDERLOIN

¼ cup vegetable oil
2 tablespoons brown sugar
2 tablespoons honey
2 tablespoons REALEMON® Lemon Juice
    from Concentrate
1 tablespoon Dijon-style mustard
2 teaspoons WYLER'S® or STEERO®
    Beef- or Chicken-Flavor Instant
    Bouillon
1 (¾- to 1-pound) pork tenderloin

In shallow dish or plastic bag, combine all
ingredients except meat; add meat. Cover;
marinate in refrigerator 6 hours or overnight.
Remove meat from marinade; grill or broil as
desired, basting frequently with marinade.
Refrigerate leftovers.

Makes 2 to 4 servings

Kamaaina Spareribs

KAMAAINA SPARERIBS

4 pounds lean pork spareribs
 Salt and pepper
1 can (20 ounces) DOLE® Crushed
 Pineapple in Juice, drained
1 cup catsup
½ cup packed brown sugar
⅓ cup red wine vinegar
¼ cup soy sauce
1 teaspoon ground ginger
½ teaspoon dry mustard
¼ teaspoon garlic powder

Have butcher cut across rib bones to make
strips 1½ inches wide. Preheat oven to 350°F.
Place ribs close together in single layer in
baking pan. Sprinkle with salt and pepper to
taste. Cover tightly with aluminum foil. Bake
1 hour. Uncover; pour off and discard drippings.

In bowl, combine remaining ingredients.
Spoon sauce over ribs. Place ribs over hot
coals. Grill 15 minutes or until ribs are tender
and glazed.   *Makes 6 servings*

BARBECUED SAUSAGE KABOBS

1 pound ECKRICH® Smoked Sausage, cut
 into 1-inch pieces
1 cup dried apricots
1 can (12 ounces) beer
½ red bell pepper, cut into 1¼-inch squares
½ green bell pepper, cut into 1¼-inch
 squares
1 Spanish onion, cut into wedges
¼ pound fresh medium mushrooms
¾ cup apricot preserves
2 tablespoons chili sauce
1 tablespoon prepared mustard
1 teaspoon Worcestershire sauce

Simmer sausage and apricots in beer in large
saucepan over low heat 10 minutes. Add
peppers to sausage mixture; remove from heat.
Let stand 10 minutes. To assemble kabobs,
thread on skewers sausage, onion, red and
green peppers, mushrooms and apricots.
Combine preserves, chili sauce, mustard and
Worcestershire sauce in small saucepan. Heat
over medium heat, stirring until blended.
Brush kabobs with sauce. Grill or broil,
4 inches from heat, 10 minutes, turning and
brushing with more sauce after 5 minutes.
Brush with remaining sauce and serve.
                      Makes 4 servings

CURRIED BEEF AND FRUIT KABOBS

1- to 1¼-pound beef top round or boneless
    beef sirloin steak, cut 1 inch thick
1 cup plain yogurt
2 teaspoons fresh lemon juice
1½ teaspoons curry powder
⅛ to ¼ teaspoon ground red pepper
1 ripe mango* (about 1 pound)
    Salt to taste

Partially freeze beef top round steak to firm;
slice into ⅛- to ¼-inch-thick strips. Combine
yogurt, lemon juice, curry powder and red
pepper. Place beef strips and marinade in
plastic bag, turning to coat. Close bag securely
and marinate in refrigerator 30 minutes,
turning occasionally. Meanwhile, soak eight
12-inch bamboo skewers in water 20 minutes.
Peel mango and cut into ¾-inch pieces.
Remove beef from marinade; discard
marinade. Thread an equal amount of beef
strips (weaving back and forth) and mango
pieces on each skewer. Place kabobs on grid
over medium coals. Grill 4 to 5 minutes,
turning once. Season with salt to taste.

Makes 4 servings

*Peaches, nectarines, plums or pineapple may
be substituted for mango. Peel and cut fruit
into ¾-inch pieces.

Note: Kabobs may also be cooked covered over
medium coals. Grill 3 to 4 minutes, turning
once.

*Favorite Recipe from **National Live Stock and Meat Board***

BIRTHDAY BURGERS

¾ cup boiling water
¼ cup bulgur (cracked wheat)
⅓ cup whole natural almonds
1 pound lean ground beef or ground turkey
¼ cup chopped green onions
1 teaspoon garlic salt
1 teaspoon dried basil leaves
4 hamburger buns
    Lettuce
    Tomato slices
    Red onion slices

Pour water over bulgur; let stand until cool.
Place almonds in single layer on baking sheet.
Bake at 350°F, 12 to 15 minutes, stirring
occasionally, until lightly toasted. Cool; chop
coarsely. Drain bulgur well. Combine bulgur,
almonds, ground beef, green onions, garlic salt
and basil; mix well. Shape into 4 patties. Grill
or broil until desired doneness. Serve on
hamburger buns with lettuce, tomatoes and red
onions. *Makes 4 servings*

*Favorite Recipe from **Almond Board of California***

Birthday Burgers

Fired-Up Poultry

Grilled chicken, Cornish hens and turkey taste great! Kabobs, burgers and boneless pieces cook in minutes. Quarters, halves and whole poultry need a slower heat and longer cooking time.

ZINGY BARBECUED CHICKEN

  1 broiler-fryer chicken, cut into parts
½ cup grapefruit juice
½ cup apple cider vinegar
½ cup vegetable oil
¼ cup chopped onion
  1 egg
½ teaspoon celery salt
½ teaspoon ground ginger
⅛ teaspoon pepper

In blender container, place all ingredients except chicken; blend 30 seconds. In small saucepan, pour blended sauce mixture and heat about 5 minutes, until slightly thick. Remove from heat; dip chicken in sauce one piece at a time, turning to thoroughly coat. Reserve sauce.

Place chicken on prepared grill, skin side up, about 8 inches from heat. Grill, turning every 10 minutes, for about 50 minutes or until fork tender and juices run clear. Brush generously with reserved sauce during last 20 minutes of grilling. Watch chicken carefully as egg in sauce may cause chicken to become too brown.   *Makes 4 servings*

Favorite Recipe from **National Broiler Council**

GRILLED TURKEY WITH VEGETABLE PIZZAZZ

1½ pounds turkey breast, cut into 2-inch pieces
  2 medium zucchini, cut into 1-inch chunks
12 large mushrooms
  1 medium red pepper, cut into 1½-inch pieces
12 jumbo pimiento-stuffed olives
  1 tablespoon vegetable oil
  1 cup pizza sauce
  1 tablespoon dried basil leaves

Thread turkey, zucchini, mushrooms, pepper and olives alternately on skewers; brush thoroughly with oil. Mix pizza sauce and basil; reserve. Grill kabobs, on uncovered grill, over medium-hot MATCH LIGHT® Charcoal Briquets about 10 minutes, turning occasionally. Baste with reserved pizza sauce and continue to grill about 15 minutes, basting and turning 2 to 3 times, until turkey is tender and vegetables are cooked.

Makes 6 servings

Zingy Barbecued Chicken

SWEET AND SPICY CHICKEN BARBECUE

1½ cups DOLE® Pineapple Orange Juice
1 cup orange marmalade
⅔ cup teriyaki sauce
½ cup packed brown sugar
½ teaspoon ground cloves
½ teaspoon ground ginger
4 frying chickens (about 2 pounds each), halved or quartered
Salt and pepper
DOLE® Pineapple Slices, drained
4 teaspoons cornstarch

In saucepan, combine juice, marmalade, teriyaki sauce, brown sugar, cloves and ginger. Heat until sugar dissolves; let cool. Sprinkle chicken with salt and pepper to taste. Place in glass baking dish. Pour juice mixture over chicken; turn to coat all sides. Marinate, covered, 2 hours in refrigerator, turning often.

Preheat oven to 350°F. Light charcoal grill. Drain chicken; reserve marinade. Bake chicken in oven 20 minutes. Arrange chicken on lightly greased grid 4 to 6 inches above glowing coals. Grill, turning and basting often with reserved marinade, 20 to 25 minutes or until meat near bone is no longer pink. Grill pineapple slices 3 minutes or until heated through.

In small saucepan, dissolve cornstarch in remaining marinade. Cook over medium heat until sauce boils and thickens. To serve, arrange chicken and pineapple on plate; spoon sauce over tops. *Makes 8 servings*

JALAPENO GRILLED CHICKEN

1 broiler-fryer chicken, quartered
2 tablespoons vegetable oil
¼ cup chopped onion
1 clove garlic, minced
1 cup catsup
2 tablespoons vinegar
1 tablespoon brown sugar
1 tablespoon minced jalapeño peppers
½ teaspoon salt
½ teaspoon dry mustard

In saucepan, heat oil to medium temperature. Add onion and garlic; cook, stirring occasionally, about 5 minutes or until onion is tender. Add catsup, vinegar, brown sugar, jalapeño peppers, salt and mustard. Cook, stirring occasionally, until mixture is blended. Place chicken, skin side up, on prepared grill about 8 inches from heat. Grill, turning every 8 to 10 minutes, about 50 minutes. Brush chicken with sauce; grill, turning and basting with sauce every 5 minutes, about 25 minutes more or until chicken is fork tender.

Makes 4 servings

*Favorite Recipe from **Delmarva Poultry Industry, Inc.***

Sweet and Spicy Chicken Barbecue

Turkey Fajitas

TURKEY FAJITAS

⅓ cup **REALEMON®** Lemon Juice from
    Concentrate
2 tablespoons vegetable oil
1 tablespoon **WYLER'S®** or **STEERO®**
    Chicken-Flavor Instant Bouillon
3 cloves garlic, finely chopped
2 fresh turkey breast tenderloins (about
    1 pound), pierced with fork
8 (8-inch) flour tortillas, warmed
    according to package directions
  Shredded lettuce and cheese, sliced ripe
     olives and green onions, salsa,
     guacamole and sour cream for garnish

In shallow dish or plastic bag, combine
ReaLemon® brand, oil, bouillon and garlic; add
turkey. Cover; marinate in refrigerator 4 hours
or overnight, turning occasionally. Remove
turkey from marinade; reserve marinade. Grill
or broil as desired, 6 inches from heat,
10 minutes per side or until no longer pink,
basting frequently with reserved marinade. Let
stand 10 minutes. Slice turkey; place on
tortillas. Top with one or more of the garnishes;
fold tortillas. Serve immediately. Refrigerate
leftovers. *Makes 4 servings*

STUFFED GRILLED GAME HENS

4 (1 to 1½ pounds each) Cornish game hens, thawed
½ cup orange juice
½ cup vegetable oil
1 garlic clove, minced
⅛ teaspoon pepper
1⅓ cups MINUTE® Rice, uncooked
1 (8-ounce) container PHILADELPHIA BRAND® Soft Cream Cheese
¼ cup golden raisins
¼ cup chopped fresh parsley
2 tablespoons orange juice
1 shallot, minced
1½ teaspoons grated orange peel
½ teaspoon salt
⅛ teaspoon pepper
Whole cooked carrots (optional)

Remove giblets; discard or save for another use. Rinse hens; pat dry.

Marinate hens in combined ½ cup orange juice, oil, garlic and ⅛ teaspoon pepper in refrigerator 30 minutes, basting occasionally.

Prepare coals for grilling.

Prepare rice according to package directions. Mix together rice and remaining ingredients except carrots in medium bowl. Remove hens from marinade, reserving marinade for basting. Stuff hens with rice mixture; close openings with skewers.

Place aluminum drip pan in center of charcoal grate under grilling rack. Arrange hot coals around drip pan.

Place hens, breast side up, on greased grill directly over drip pan. Grill, covered, 1 hour and 15 minutes to 1 hour and 30 minutes or until tender, brushing frequently with reserved marinade.

Serve with whole carrots, if desired.

Makes 4 servings

TASTY TACO CHICKEN GRILL

1 broiler-fryer chicken, cut into parts
1 small onion, minced
1 can (8 ounces) Spanish-style tomato sauce
1 can (4 ounces) taco sauce
¼ cup molasses
2 tablespoons vinegar
1 tablespoon vegetable oil
1 teaspoon salt
½ teaspoon oregano leaves
⅛ teaspoon pepper
½ cup shredded Monterey Jack cheese

In small saucepan, make sauce by mixing together onion, tomato sauce, taco sauce, molasses, vinegar, oil, salt, oregano and pepper; bring sauce to a boil. Remove from heat and cool 2 minutes. In large shallow dish, place chicken; pour sauce over chicken. Cover and marinate in refrigerator at least 1 hour.

Drain chicken; reserve sauce. Place chicken on prepared grill, skin side up, about 8 inches from heat. Grill, turning every 10 minutes, about 50 minutes or until fork tender and juices run clear. Brush generously with reserved sauce during last 20 minutes of grilling. When chicken is done, place on platter; sprinkle with cheese.

Makes 4 servings

*Favorite recipe from **National Broiler Council***

TURKEY BURGERS

1 pound ground fresh turkey
¼ cup BENNETT'S® Chili Sauce
1 teaspoon WYLER'S® or STEERO® Chicken-Flavor Instant Bouillon

Combine ingredients; shape into patties. Grill, broil or pan-fry until no longer pink in center. Refrigerate leftovers. *Makes 4 servings*

Hot and Spicy Barbecue Drumsticks

Wrap each drumstick in heavy-duty aluminum foil, leaving room for steam expansion and keeping dull side of foil out. Grill over a single layer of slow coals, 1 hour for large drumsticks and 45 minutes for small drumsticks, turning every 15 minutes and adding additional charcoal as needed to maintain temperature.

Meanwhile, prepare barbecue sauce by combining remaining ingredients in small bowl. Remove aluminum foil from drumsticks and continue grilling an additional 30 minutes over slow coals, basting twice on each side with sauce and turning drumsticks after 15 minutes.   *Makes 8 servings (½ large or 1 small drumstick each)*

*Favorite Recipe from **California Turkey Industry Board***

HOT AND SPICY BARBECUE DRUMSTICKS

> 4 large California-Grown Turkey drumsticks, about 1½ pounds each, *or* 8 small California-Grown Turkey drumsticks, about ¾ pound each
> 1 can (8 ounces) tomato sauce
> Juice from 1 fresh lemon
> 4 large cloves garlic, crushed
> 2 tablespoons sugar
> 1 teaspoon chili powder
> 1 teaspoon salt
> 1 teaspoon Worcestershire sauce
> ¼ teaspoon pepper
> ¼ teaspoon hot pepper sauce

MID-EASTERN TANGY CHICKEN

> 1 broiler-fryer chicken, quartered
> 1 tablespoon butter or margarine
> ¼ cup minced onion
> 1 clove garlic, minced
> 1 cup plain yogurt
> 1 teaspoon salt
> ½ teaspoon ground turmeric
> ½ teaspoon chili powder
> 3 tablespoons white wine

In small saucepan, make sauce by melting butter over medium heat. Add onion and garlic; stir and cook about 3 minutes or until onion is clear and soft. Remove from heat and stir in yogurt, salt, turmeric and chili powder. Let cool 2 minutes; stir in white wine. In large shallow dish, place chicken quarters. Pour sauce over chicken; cover and marinate in refrigerator at least 1 hour.

Remove chicken from sauce; reserve sauce. Place chicken on prepared grill, skin side up, about 8 inches from heat. Grill, turning every 15 minutes, for about 60 minutes or until fork tender and juices run clear. Brush generously with reserved sauce during last 30 minutes of grilling.   *Makes 4 servings*

*Favorite Recipe from **National Broiler Council***

GRILLED TURKEY WITH WALNUT PESTO

1 (4- to 5½-pound) turkey breast
Walnut Pesto Sauce (recipe follows)

Prepare coals for grilling. Place aluminum drip pan in center of charcoal grate under grilling rack. Arrange hot coals around drip pan. Place turkey on greased grill. Grill, covered, 1½ to 2 hours or until internal temperature reaches 170°F. Slice turkey; serve with Walnut Pesto Sauce. Garnish with red and yellow pear-shaped cherry tomatoes, fresh chives and basil leaves, if desired.   *Makes 12 servings*

WALNUT PESTO SAUCE

1 (8-ounce) container PHILADELPHIA BRAND® "Light" Pasteurized Process Cream Cheese Product
1 (7-ounce) container refrigerated prepared pesto
½ cup finely chopped walnuts, toasted
⅓ cup milk
1 garlic clove, minced
⅛ teaspoon ground red pepper

Stir together all ingredients in small bowl until well blended. Serve chilled or at room temperature.

Grilled Turkey with Walnut Pesto

MEXICAN CHICKEN WITH SPICY BACON

  2 serrano chili peppers
  2 cloves garlic
    Dash ground cloves
    Dash ground cinnamon
  4 slices bacon, partially cooked
  1 whole roasting chicken (3½ to 4 pounds)
    Cherry tomatoes and serrano chili
      peppers for garnish (optional)

Remove stems from peppers. Slit open; remove seeds and ribs. Finely chop peppers and garlic. Place in small bowl. Stir in cloves and cinnamon. Cut bacon into 1-inch pieces.

Lift skin layer of chicken at neck cavity. Insert hand, lifting skin from meat along breast, thigh and drumstick. Using small metal spatula, spread pepper mixture evenly over meat, under skin. Place layer of bacon pieces over pepper mixture. Skewer neck skin to back. Tie legs securely to tail and twist wing tips under back of chicken. Insert meat thermometer in center of thigh muscle, not touching bone.

Arrange medium-hot KINGSFORD® Briquets around drip pan. Place chicken, breast side up, over drip pan. Cover grill and cook about 1 hour or until meat thermometer registers 185°F. Garnish with cherry tomatoes and serrano chili peppers, if desired.   *Makes 4 servings*

Mexican Chicken with Spicy Bacon

HERBED LIME CHICKEN

½ cup vegetable oil
⅓ cup lime juice
¼ cup chopped onion
2 cloves garlic, crushed
1 teaspoon TABASCO® Pepper Sauce
¾ teaspoon dried rosemary leaves, crumbled
½ teaspoon dried marjoram leaves, crumbled
½ teaspoon salt
2 to 3 pounds chicken pieces

In dish, combine oil, lime juice, onion, garlic, Tabasco® sauce, rosemary, marjoram and salt. Place chicken in large shallow dish or plastic bag; pour marinade over chicken. Cover and marinate in refrigerator overnight; turn chicken occasionally.

Drain chicken; reserve marinade. Place chicken on grid about 5 inches from heat. Grill about 20 minutes per side or until done, brushing with reserved marinade several times. *Makes 4 servings*

BEER-BASTED CHICKEN LEGS

4 whole broiler-fryer chicken legs (thigh and drumstick attached)
¾ cup chili sauce
½ cup beer
1 tablespoon dark brown sugar
1 tablespoon Worcestershire sauce
2 teaspoons prepared horseradish
½ teaspoon salt

In small bowl, mix together chili sauce, beer, brown sugar, Worcestershire sauce, prepared horseradish and salt. Place chicken, skin side up, on prepared grill about 8 inches from heat. Grill, turning every 10 minutes, about 35 minutes. Brush chicken with sauce; grill, turning and basting with sauce every 5 minutes, about 20 minutes more or until chicken is fork tender. *Makes 4 servings*

*Favorite Recipe from **Delmarva Poultry Industry, Inc.***

California Turkey Skewers

CALIFORNIA TURKEY SKEWERS

California Glaze (recipe follows)
1 California-Grown Turkey breast half, about 3 pounds
1 package (9 ounces) frozen artichoke hearts, thawed
8 ears of corn, blanched, cut into chunks*

Prepare California Glaze. Cut turkey into 1½-inch cubes. Thread turkey, artichoke hearts and corn chunks on skewers. Barbecue or broil 15 to 20 minutes, brushing frequently with California Glaze; turn often.

Makes 8 to 10 servings

California Glaze: In saucepan combine ½ cup orange juice, 2 tablespoons *each* firmly packed brown sugar, vinegar, lemon juice and honey, 1 tablespoon cornstarch, 1 teaspoon salt, ½ teaspoon *each* dry mustard and grated orange peel and ¼ teaspoon dried tarragon leaves, crushed. Bring to a boil.

*Thawed, frozen ears of corn may be used.

*Favorite Recipe from **California Turkey Industry Board***

BUFFALO TURKEY KABOBS

⅔ cup HELLMANN'S® or BEST FOODS®
   Real, Light or Cholesterol Free
   Reduced Calorie Mayonnaise, divided
1 teaspoon hot pepper sauce
1½ pounds boneless turkey breast, cut into
   1-inch cubes
2 red bell peppers *or* 1 red and 1 yellow
   bell pepper, cut into 1-inch squares
2 medium onions, cut into wedges
¼ cup (1 ounce) crumbed blue cheese
2 tablespoons milk
1 medium stalk celery, minced
1 medium carrot, minced

In medium bowl, combine ⅓ cup of the
mayonnaise and the hot pepper sauce. Stir in
turkey. Cover and marinate in refrigerator
20 minutes. Drain turkey; discard marinade.
On 6 skewers, thread turkey, peppers and
onions. Grill or broil, 5 inches from heat,
brushing with remaining mayonnaise mixture
and turning frequently, 12 to 15 minutes.
Meanwhile, in small bowl blend remaining
⅓ cup mayonnaise with blue cheese and milk.
Stir in celery and carrot. Serve with kabobs.
                              Makes 6 servings

Note: For best results, use Real Mayonnaise. If
using Light or Cholesterol Free Reduced
Calorie Mayonnaise, use sauce the same day.

SPICY THAI CHICKEN

¾ cup canned cream of coconut
3 tablespoons lime juice
3 tablespoons soy sauce
8 sprigs cilantro
3 large cloves garlic
3 large green onions, cut up
3 anchovy fillets
1 teaspoon TABASCO® Pepper Sauce
2 whole boneless skinless chicken breasts,
   cut into halves (about 1½ pounds)

In blender container or food processor,
combine cream of coconut, lime juice, soy
sauce, cilantro, garlic, green onions, anchovies
and Tabasco® sauce. Cover; process until
smooth. Place chicken in large shallow dish or
plastic bag; add marinade. Cover; refrigerate at
least 2 hours, turning chicken occasionally.

Drain chicken; reserve marinade. Place
chicken on grill about 5 inches from source of
heat. Brush generously with marinade. Grill
5 minutes. Turn chicken; brush with reserved
marinade. Grill 5 minutes longer or until
chicken is cooked. Heat any remaining
marinade to a boil; serve as dipping sauce for
chicken.   *Makes 4 servings*

GRILLED CHICKEN
POLYNESIAN TREAT

12 broiler-fryer chicken thighs
 2 tablespoons butter or margarine
 1 small onion, minced
¾ cup vinegar
¼ cup soy sauce
¼ cup plum jam
¼ teaspoon salt
 1 bay leaf
 3 large pineapples, cut lengthwise into
   halves
 2 large green peppers, sliced into rings

In small saucepan, melt butter over medium
heat; add onion. Stir and cook about 3 minutes
or until onion is clear and soft. Add vinegar,
soy sauce and plum jam. Bring mixture to a
boil, stirring constantly. Remove from heat and
stir in salt and bay leaf. In large shallow dish,
place chicken thighs; pour hot sauce over
chicken. Cover and marinate in refrigerator at
least 1 hour.

Remove chicken from sauce; reserve sauce.
Place chicken thighs on prepared grill, skin
side up, about 8 inches from heat. Grill about
15 minutes or until brown on one side. Turn
and continue grilling 15 minutes longer.
Chicken is done when fork tender and juices
run clear. Brush generously with reserved
sauce during entire grilling time. Serve chicken
thighs in scooped out pineapple halves and top
with green pepper rings.   *Makes 6 servings*

*Favorite Recipe from **National Broiler Council***

Buffalo Turkey Kabobs

COOL GRILLED CHICKEN SALAD

1 pound boneless, skinless chicken breasts
¼ cup lemon juice
2 tablespoons olive or vegetable oil
1 teaspoon dried tarragon leaves, crushed
¾ teaspoon LAWRY'S® Garlic Salt
1 quart salad greens, torn into bite-size pieces
6 medium red potatoes, cooked, cooled and cut into chunks
1 cup shredded carrot

Rinse chicken and place in resealable plastic bag. In small bowl, combine lemon juice, oil, tarragon and Garlic Salt; blend well. Pour marinade over chicken; seal bag and refrigerate 30 to 45 minutes or overnight. Drain chicken; reserve marinade. Grill or broil chicken 4 minutes on each side, basting with reserved marinade, until golden and cooked through. Cool and cut into strips. Line individual plates with salad greens. Arrange potato chunks, carrot and chicken on top.

Makes 4 main-dish servings

Hint: For a more colorful salad, add sliced tomatoes or shredded red cabbage.

SPICY BARBECUED WINGETTES

12 PERDUE OVEN STUFFER Wingettes
⅔ cup cider vinegar
⅓ cup vegetable oil
½ teaspoon hot pepper sauce
¼ teaspoon crushed dried red pepper
1 clove garlic, minced or pressed

Rinse wingettes and pat dry; place in shallow dish. In small saucepan over medium heat, stir together remaining ingredients. Cook about 5 minutes or until mixture is hot; pour over wingettes. Cover; refrigerate several hours or overnight.

Prepare outdoor grill for cooking or preheat broiler. Remove wingettes from marinade; reserve marinade. Grill 6 inches from source of heat or broil indoors 25 to 35 minutes, turning and basting frequently with reserved marinade. Let stand 5 minutes before serving.

Makes 6 servings

CHICKEN KABOBS WITH PEANUT SAUCE

2 whole broiler-fryer chicken breasts, halved, boned, skinned, cut into 1-inch pieces
¼ cup finely chopped onion
2 tablespoons white wine
2 tablespoons soy sauce
1 tablespoon brown sugar
1 tablespoon vegetable oil
½ teaspoon ground coriander
1 clove garlic, crushed
2 cans (8 ounces each) pineapple chunks in natural juice, drained
2 red or green peppers, halved, cored, cut into 1-inch pieces
Peanut Sauce (recipe follows)

In shallow, nonmetallic dish, mix together onion, wine, soy sauce, brown sugar, oil, coriander and garlic. Add chicken, stirring to coat. Cover and marinate in refrigerator, stirring occasionally, 1 hour. Drain chicken; reserve marinade. On each of 8 skewers, thread chicken, pineapple and peppers. Place chicken on prepared grill about 8 inches from heat. Grill, turning and basting frequently with reserved marinade, about 20 minutes or until chicken is fork tender. Serve with Peanut Sauce.

Makes 4 servings

Peanut Sauce: In saucepan, place ½ cup chunky peanut butter, ¼ cup finely chopped onion, ¼ cup canned cream of coconut, ¼ cup water, 2 tablespoons soy sauce, 1 tablespoon brown sugar and ¼ tablespoon crushed red pepper flakes. Heat, stirring, until mixture boils.

Makes about 1¼ cups

*Favorite Recipe from **Delmarva Poultry Industry, Inc.***

Cool Grilled Chicken Salad

Grilled Cornish Game Hens

GRILLED CORNISH GAME HENS

  2 Cornish game hens (1 to 1½ pounds each)
  3 tablespoons olive oil
  ⅓ cup lemon juice
  1 tablespoon black peppercorns, coarsely crushed
  ½ teaspoon salt
    Fresh rosemary sprigs (optional)

Split hens lengthwise. Rinse hen halves; pat dry with paper toweling.

For marinade, in small bowl combine olive oil, lemon juice, peppercorns and salt. Place hen halves in large plastic bag. Set in bowl. Pour marinade over hens. Close bag and refrigerate several hours or overnight, turning hen halves occasionally to coat with marinade.

Arrange medium-hot KINGSFORD® Briquets around drip pan. Just before grilling, add a rosemary sprig to coals. Remove hens from marinade; reserve marinade. Place hens, skin side up, over drip pan. Cover grill and cook 45 minutes or until thigh moves easily and juices run clear. Baste with reserved marinade occasionally. Garnish with rosemary sprigs, if desired. *Makes 4 servings*

BARBECUED CHICKEN

  1 cup chicken broth
  ¼ cup catsup
  2 tablespoons vinegar
  2 tablespoons Worcestershire sauce
  2 tablespoons finely chopped onion
  1 teaspoon dry mustard
  ½ teaspoon garlic salt
  ½ teaspoon salt
  ¼ teaspoon pepper
  1 broiler-fryer chicken (2 to 3 pounds),
    quartered

Combine all ingredients, except chicken, in small saucepan. Bring to boil; cool slightly. Place chicken in shallow glass dish. Pour warm sauce over chicken; cover and refrigerate at least 2 hours. Drain chicken; reserve marinade. Grill chicken, skin side up, on uncovered grill, over hot KINGSFORD® Briquets 40 to 55 minutes, basting often with reserved marinade and turning frequently, until chicken is fork tender.   *Makes 4 to 5 servings*

CHICKEN VEGETABLE KABOBS

  ½ cup WISH-BONE® Italian Dressing
  ¼ cup dry white wine
  1 pound boneless chicken breasts, cubed
  1 medium zucchini, cut into ½-inch pieces
  1 large green pepper, cut into chunks

In large shallow baking dish, blend Italian dressing with wine. Add chicken and vegetables and turn to coat. Cover and marinate in refrigerator, turning occasionally, at least 2 hours. Remove chicken and vegetables; reserve marinade.

Onto skewers; thread chicken and vegetables. Grill or broil, turning and basting frequently with reserved marinade, until chicken is done.
          Makes about 4 servings

CHILI TOMATO GRILLED CHICKEN

  6 broiler-fryer chicken quarters
  2 tablespoons vegetable oil
  ½ cup finely chopped onion
  1 clove garlic, minced
  1 chicken bouillon cube
  ½ cup hot water
  1 bottle (8 ounces) taco sauce *or* 1 can
    (8 ounces) tomato sauce
  1 teaspoon salt
  ¼ teaspoon dried oregano leaves
  2 tablespoons vinegar
  1 tablespoon prepared mustard
  3 teaspoons mild chili powder, divided

In small skillet, place oil and heat to medium temperature. Add onion and garlic; stir and cook about 3 minutes or until clear and soft. Dissolve bouillon cube in hot water; add bouillon to skillet, along with taco sauce, salt, oregano, vinegar and mustard. Dip chicken into sauce mixture; then sprinkle 2 teaspoons of the chili powder on all sides of chicken. Add remaining 1 teaspoon of chili powder to sauce; bring to a boil and remove from heat. Redip each quarter in sauce. Place chicken on prepared grill, skin side up, about 8 inches from heat. Grill, turning every 15 minutes, for about 60 minutes or until fork tender and juices run clear. Brush generously with sauce during last 30 minutes of grilling.
          Makes 6 servings

*Favorite Recipe from **National Broiler Council***

Grilled Seafood

Fish and shellfish cook quickly and deliciously on the grill. In just minutes you can serve your guests fork-tender fish and melt-in-the-mouth scallops or shrimp.

SALMON STEAKS IN ORANGE-HONEY MARINADE

⅓ cup orange juice
⅓ cup soy sauce
3 tablespoons peanut oil
3 tablespoons catsup
1 tablespoon honey
½ teaspoon ground ginger
1 clove garlic, crushed
4 salmon steaks (about 6 ounces each)

In 1-quart measure, mix all ingredients except salmon steaks. Place salmon steaks in shallow glass dish. Pour marinade over salmon steaks; cover and marinate in refrigerator 1 hour. Drain salmon; reserve marinade. Grill salmon, on uncovered grill, 6 inches above hot KINGSFORD® Briquets 5 minutes. Carefully turn salmon steaks. Brush with reserved marinade and grill 5 minutes longer or until salmon flakes easily when tested with fork.

Makes 4 servings

SEAFOOD KABOBS

⅓ cup pineapple juice
⅓ cup REALEMON® Lemon Juice from Concentrate
2 tablespoons vegetable oil
1 to 2 tablespoons brown sugar
1 teaspoon grated orange rind
¼ teaspoon ground cinnamon
¾ pound large raw shrimp, peeled and deveined
½ pound sea scallops
1 cup melon chunks or balls
1 medium avocado, peeled, seeded and cut into chunks

In large shallow dish or plastic bag, combine juices, oil, sugar, rind and cinnamon; add seafood and melon. Cover; marinate in refrigerator 4 hours or overnight. Place shrimp, scallops, melon and avocado on skewers. Grill or broil 3 to 6 minutes or until shrimp are pink and scallops are opaque, basting frequently with marinade. Refrigerate leftovers.

Makes 4 servings

Top to bottom: Salmon Steaks in Orange-Honey Marinade, Seafood Kabobs

MAGIC GRILLED FISH

6 (½-inch-thick) firm-fleshed fish fillets
(8 to 10 ounces each), such as redfish,
pompano, tilefish, red snapper, or
salmon or tuna steaks
¾ cup (1½ sticks) unsalted butter, melted
3 tablespoons plus 2 teaspoons CHEF
PAUL PRUDHOMME 'S BLACKENED
REDFISH MAGIC®

Heat grill as hot as possible and have flames reaching above grid before putting fish on grill. Add dry wood chunks to glowing coals to make fire hotter.

Dip each fillet in melted butter so that both sides are well coated, then sprinkle Blackened Redfish Magic generously and evenly on both sides of fillets, patting it in by hand. Place fillets directly over flame on very hot grill and pour 1 teaspoon of the melted butter on top of each. (Be careful; butter may flare up.) Cook, uncovered, directly in flames until underside looks blackened, about 2 minutes. (Time will vary according to each fillet's thickness and heat of grill.) Turn fish over and grill until cooked through, about 2 minutes more. Serve piping hot with assorted grilled vegetables.

Makes 6 servings

Note: Do not prepare this recipe indoors.

Magic Grilled Fish

Shrimp and Steak Kabobs

SHRIMP AND STEAK KABOBS

½ cup vegetable oil
¼ cup REALEMON® Lemon Juice from
Concentrate
1 teaspoon dried oregano leaves
½ teaspoon dried basil leaves
1 clove garlic, finely chopped
½ pound medium raw shrimp, peeled and
deveined
½ pound boneless beef sirloin, cut into
cubes
Zucchini, onion and red or yellow bell
pepper chunks

In shallow dish or plastic bag, combine oil,
ReaLemon® brand, oregano, basil and garlic;
add shrimp and meat. Cover; marinate in
refrigerator 3 to 4 hours. Skewer shrimp and
meat with vegetables. Grill or broil as desired,
basting frequently with marinade.
Makes 16 appetizer or 4 main-dish servings

Tip: One-half pound of scallops can be
substituted for sirloin.

LAKESIDE LOBSTER TAILS

4 (1-pound) cleaned lobster tails with shells
Herb Wine Sauce (recipe follows)
Lemon wedges (optional)

Prepare coals for grilling. Cut lobster tails
through center of back with knife or kitchen
shears; split open. Place lobster, shell side
down, on greased grill over hot coals (coals will
be glowing). Grill, covered, 5 to 8 minutes on
each side or until shell is bright red and lobster
meat is white. Serve with Herb Wine Sauce.
Garnish with lemon wedges, if desired.
Makes 4 servings

HERB WINE SAUCE

1 (8-ounce) container PHILADELPHIA
BRAND® Soft Cream Cheese with
Herb & Garlic
¼ cup dry white wine
2 green onions, thinly sliced
½ teaspoon salt

Stir together ingredients in small bowl until
well blended.

"Grilled" Tuna with Vegetables in Herb Butter

"GRILLED" TUNA WITH VEGETABLES IN HERB BUTTER

1 can (12½ ounces) STARKIST® Tuna,
  drained and broken into chunks
1 cup slivered red or green bell pepper
1 cup slivered yellow squash or zucchini
1 cup slivered carrots
1 cup pea pods, cut crosswise into halves
4 green onions, cut into ½-inch slices
¼ cup butter or margarine, melted
1 tablespoon lemon or lime juice
1 clove garlic, minced
2 teaspoons dried tarragon leaves, crushed
1 teaspoon dried dill weed
  Salt and pepper to taste

On four 12×18-inch pieces heavy-duty aluminum foil mound tuna, bell pepper, squash, carrots, pea pods and onions, dividing evenly. For herb butter, in small bowl stir together butter, lemon juice, garlic, tarragon and dill weed. Drizzle mixture over tuna and vegetables. Sprinkle with salt and pepper. Fold edges of each foil square together to make 4 individual packets.

To grill, place foil packets about 4 inches above hot coals. Grill 10 to 12 minutes, or until heated through, turning packet over halfway through grill time.

To bake, place foil packets on baking sheet. Bake in preheated 450°F oven 15 to 20 minutes, or until heated through.

To serve, cut an "X" on top of each packet; peel back foil. Garnish as desired.

Makes 4 servings

SALMON WITH MUSTARD DILL SAUCE

¼ cup mayonnaise or salad dressing
¼ cup BORDEN® or MEADOW GOLD®
    Sour Cream
1 tablespoon sliced green onion
1 teaspoon Dijon-style mustard
⅓ cup plus 1 teaspoon REALEMON®
    Lemon Juice from Concentrate
1½ teaspoons dried dill weed
4 (1-inch-thick) salmon steaks (about
    1½ pounds)

In small bowl, combine mayonnaise, sour cream, green onion, mustard, *1 teaspoon* ReaLemon® brand and *½ teaspoon* dill weed. Cover; chill. In shallow dish or plastic bag, combine remaining *⅓ cup* ReaLemon® brand and *1 teaspoon* dill weed; add fish. Cover; marinate in refrigerator 1 hour. Grill, broil or bake as desired, brushing frequently with marinade. Serve with mustard dill sauce. Refrigerate leftovers.   *Makes 4 servings*

HOT GRILLED TROUT

¼ cup lemon juice
2 tablespoons butter or margarine, melted
2 tablespoons olive oil
2 tablespoons chopped parsley
2 tablespoons sesame seeds
1 tablespoon TABASCO® Pepper Sauce
½ teaspoon ground ginger
½ teaspoon salt
4 brook trout (about 1 pound each)

In shallow dish, combine lemon juice, butter, oil, parsley, sesame seeds, Tabasco® sauce, ginger and salt. With fork, pierce skin of trout. Coat fish, inside and out, with marinade. Cover and refrigerate 30 to 60 minutes.

Drain fish; reserve marinade. Place fish in oiled grill basket; brush with reserved marinade. Cook 4 inches from hot coals 10 minutes or until fish flakes easily when tested with fork, turning and brushing with marinade once.   *Makes 4 servings*

Salmon with Mustard Dill Sauce

SWORDFISH WITH LEEK CREAM

4 (1 to 1½ pounds total) swordfish steaks
2 tablespoons olive oil
Leek Cream (recipe follows)

Prepare coals for grilling. Brush fish with oil.
Place fish on greased grill over hot coals (coals
will be glowing). Grill, uncovered, 3 to
4 minutes on each side or until fish flakes
easily when tested with fork. Serve with Leek
Cream.   *Makes 4 servings*

LEEK CREAM

1 leek, cut into 1-inch strips
2 tablespoons PARKAY® Margarine
1 (3-ounce) package PHILADELPHIA
    BRAND® Cream Cheese, cubed
3 tablespoons dry white wine
2 tablespoons chopped fresh parsley
½ teaspoon garlic salt
¼ teaspoon pepper

Sauté leeks in margarine in medium skillet
until tender. Add remaining ingredients; stir
over low heat until cream cheese is melted.

DEVILED TROUT FILLETS

2 pounds trout fillets, fresh or frozen
½ cup chili sauce
2 tablespoons vegetable oil
2 tablespoons prepared mustard
2 tablespoons cream-style prepared
    horseradish
1 tablespoon Worcestershire sauce
½ teaspoon salt

Thaw fish, if frozen. Place fish on well-greased
grid. Mix remaining ingredients in small bowl
until blended. Spread sauce evenly over fish.
Grill, 6 inches from medium hot coals, 5 to
8 minutes or until fish begins to flake when
tested with a fork.   *Makes 6 servings*

Favorite recipe from **National Fisheries Institute**

SHRIMP IN FOIL

1 pound medium raw shrimp, peeled and
    deveined
1 cup sliced fresh mushrooms
¼ cup sliced green onions
2 tablespoons margarine or butter
¼ cup REALEMON® Lemon Juice from
    Concentrate
½ to 1 teaspoon dried dill weed
½ teaspoon salt
⅛ teaspoon pepper
2 tablespoons chopped parsley

On 4 large heavy-duty aluminum foil squares,
place equal amounts of shrimp, mushrooms
and green onions. Melt margarine; add
ReaLemon® brand, dill weed, salt and pepper.
Pour equal amounts over shrimp. Sprinkle with
parsley. Fold and seal foil securely around
shrimp. Grill 8 minutes or until shrimp are
pink or bake in preheated 400° oven 12 to
15 minutes. Refrigerate leftovers.
                                Makes 4 servings

GRILLED SALMON WITH CUCUMBER SAUCE

¾ cup HELLMANN'S® or BEST FOODS®
    Real, Light or Cholesterol Free
    Reduced Calorie Mayonnaise
¼ cup snipped fresh dill *or* 1 tablespoon
    dried dill weed
1 tablespoon lemon juice
6 salmon steaks (4 ounces each),
    ¾ inch thick
1 small cucumber, seeded and chopped
½ cup chopped radishes
    Lemon wedges

In medium bowl combine mayonnaise, dill and
lemon juice; reserve ½ cup for sauce. Brush
fish steaks with remaining mayonnaise
mixture. Grill 6 inches from heat, turning and
brushing frequently with mayonnaise mixture,
6 to 8 minutes or until fish is firm but moist.
Stir cucumber and radishes into reserved
mayonnaise mixture. Serve fish with
cucumber sauce and lemon wedges.
                                Makes 6 servings

Swordfish with Leek Cream

SEAFOOD-VEGETABLE KABOBS

2 dozen large sea scallops
1 dozen medium shrimp, shelled and
   deveined
2 red or yellow peppers, cut into 2-inch
   pieces
1 can (8½ ounces) artichoke hearts,
   drained
¼ cup olive or vegetable oil
¼ cup lime juice

Combine all ingredients in bowl; toss gently.
Thread scallops, shrimp, peppers and
artichokes onto skewers; reserve marinade.
Lightly oil grid. Grill kabobs, on uncovered
grill, over low KINGSFORD® Briquets 6 to
8 minutes or until scallops turn opaque and
shrimp turn pink. Turn kabobs twice during
grilling; brush with reserved marinade.

Makes 6 servings

EASY BROILED ALBACORE

1 tablespoon vegetable oil
2 tablespoons lime juice
1 teaspoon Worcestershire sauce
1½ teaspoons dry mustard
1½ pounds skinned albacore tuna steaks or
   loin cuts, 1 inch thick
2 tablespoons grated lime peel

Combine oil, lime juice, Worcestershire sauce
and mustard in small bowl to make basting
sauce. Arrange albacore on well-greased grid.
Baste with sauce. Grill, 4 to 5 inches from
medium-hot coals, 6 to 8 minutes, turning fish
halfway through cooking time and basting
frequently. Albacore should be pink in center
when removed from heat. Top with lime peel.

Makes 4 servings

*Favorite Recipe from **National Fisheries Institute***

Seafood-Vegetable Kabobs

Grilled Rainbow Trout with Caponata Relish

GRILLED RAINBOW TROUT WITH CAPONATA RELISH

2 tablespoons olive oil
1 to 2 cloves garlic, crushed
1 cup peeled and chopped eggplant or
   sliced mushrooms
½ cup chopped bell peppers (mix of green
   and yellow peppers)
½ cup chopped tomatoes
2 tablespoons sliced ripe olives
1 tablespoon capers
1 teaspoon balsamic or red wine vinegar
4 CLEAR SPRINGS® Brand Idaho
   Rainbow Trout fillets (4 ounces each)

In small saucepan, heat oil over medium heat; sauté garlic 1 minute. Add eggplant and peppers; stir quickly to coat. Sauté 5 minutes until softened. Add tomatoes, olives, capers and vinegar. Continue cooking 5 minutes longer; hold on very low heat. Over hot coals, place trout fillets, flesh side down, on oiled grid and cook about 2 minutes. Gently turn trout with spatula; continue cooking 2 minutes longer or until fish flakes easily with fork. Serve immediately topped with 2 tablespoons of caponata relish.   *Makes 4 servings*

TERIYAKI FISH FILLETS

1 can (20 ounces) DOLE® Pineapple
   Chunks in Juice
1 clove garlic, pressed
2 tablespoons slivered fresh ginger root
1 tablespoon minced green onion
5 teaspoons teriyaki sauce
1 teaspoon white vinegar
1 pound sole fillets
2 teaspoons cornstarch
1 teaspoon minced fresh ginger root
1 teaspoon sesame oil

Measure 2 tablespoons juice from pineapple can; mix with garlic, slivered ginger, onion, 3 teaspoons teriyaki sauce and the vinegar. Arrange fish in shallow dish. Pour marinade over fish. Refrigerate 10 minutes. Drain fish; reserve marinade. Arrange fish on oiled grid. Brush with reserved marinade. Grill or broil 6 inches from heat 5 to 6 minutes or until fish flakes easily with fork.

In saucepan, combine remaining 2 teaspoons teriyaki sauce, undrained pineapple and remaining ingredients. Cook, stirring, until sauce boils and thickens. Serve with fish.
                                         Makes 4 servings

Shark Steaks in Beer Marinade

SHARK STEAKS IN BEER MARINADE

2 pounds shark steaks or fillets, fresh or
  frozen
⅔ cup beer
⅓ cup vegetable oil
1 teaspoon salt
¼ teaspoon garlic powder
¼ teaspoon pepper
1 teaspoon prepared mustard
2 tablespoons butter or margarine
½ teaspoon paprika
4 cups sliced onions
1 cup sour cream, warmed
½ teaspoon prepared horseradish

Thaw fish, if frozen. Combine beer, oil, salt, garlic powder, pepper and mustard in shallow dish. Add fish. Marinate in refrigerator, covered, at least 30 minutes. Remove fish from marinade; discard marinade. Arrange fish on well-greased grid. Grill, 4 inches from medium-hot coals, 8 to 10 minutes or until fish flakes easily when tested with fork, turning fish over halfway through cooking.

Melt butter in medium saucepan over medium-high heat. Stir in paprika; add onions. Sauté until onions are tender but not brown. Combine warm sour cream and horseradish in small bowl. To serve, top each fish steak with onions and a spoonful of sour cream mixture.

Makes 6 servings

*Favorite Recipe from **Florida Department of National Resources***

CITRUS GRILLED WHOLE FISH WITH LIME BUTTER

1 whole fish (3 to 8 pounds), such as
   salmon, bluefish, red snapper or
   trout, with head and tail removed, if
   desired
Vegetable oil
Freshly ground black pepper
1 teaspoon grated lemon peel
1 or 2 limes, thinly sliced
1 or 2 lemons, thinly sliced
Lime wedges
Lime Butter (recipe follows)

Brush fish cavity with oil and season with pepper and lemon peel. Overlap alternating lime and lemon slices; place in cavity of fish. Oil outside of fish thoroughly. Measure thickness of fish at its thickest part. Place fish in oiled fish basket. Or, make fish-turning handles: Fold two 18×12-inch pieces of heavy-duty foil in half 3 times to make two 18×1½-inch strips. Place fish on its side on foil strips; wrap strips around fish and twist each at the belly sides.

Bank hot coals on both sides of grill. Oil grid and place 4 to 6 inches above coals. Place fish on grid; grill 10 to 12 minutes per inch of thickness. Baste with oil and turn fish over halfway through cooking time (re-oil grid). Fish is cooked when it flakes easily when tested with fork and internal temperature is 140°F.

Place fish on warm serving platter. Lift off top layer of skin, if desired. Cut top of fish lengthwise along backbone. Slide wide spatula between flesh and ribs and lift off each serving. When top half of fish has been served, lift and remove backbone. Cut down to skin to serve remaining half. Serve with lime wedges and Lime Butter. *Makes 6 to 8 servings for a 4-pound round fish*

Lime Butter: Combine ½ cup softened butter or margarine, 2 to 3 tablespoons fresh lime juice, 1 teaspoon grated lime peel and a dash of salt in bowl or food processor. Beat or process until soft and light. *Makes about ½ cup*

*Favorite Recipe from **National Fisheries Institute***

GRILLED LEMON-MUSTARD TROUT

¼ cup fresh lemon juice
1 tablespoon Dijon-style mustard
2 cloves garlic, minced
⅛ teaspoon salt
⅛ teaspoon freshly ground white pepper
2 tablespoons olive oil
2 tablespoons chopped fresh chives
6 to 8 CLEAR SPRINGS® Brand Idaho
   Rainbow Trout fillets (4 ounces each)

Combine lemon juice, mustard, garlic, salt and pepper; gradually whisk in oil. Stir in chives and pour marinade over trout. Marinate trout in refrigerator about 30 minutes.

Drain trout; reserve marinade. Over hot coals, place trout, flesh side down, on oiled grill and cook about 2 minutes. Use 2 spatulas to gently turn trout; cook about 2 minutes longer until done. Serve immediately. If desired, bring reserved marinade to a boil and cook 1 minute; serve with grilled trout.
Makes 4 to 6 servings

ORIENTAL BARBECUED SCALLOPS

½ cup soy sauce
1 tablespoon sugar
2 tablespoons white wine
2 teaspoons lemon juice
1 teaspoon sesame oil
1 clove garlic, crushed
3 to 4 pounds large sea scallops

Mix all ingredients, except scallops, in large bowl. Add scallops; cover and refrigerate 1 hour. Thread scallops on skewers; reserve marinade. Grill scallops, on uncovered grill, over medium-hot KINGSFORD® Briquets 10 minutes or until scallops turn opaque, turning and brushing with reserved marinade.
Makes 6 to 8 servings

Salads & Extras

Potato, vegetable, fruit and gelatin—all the great salad combinations for outdoor eating are here. The extras are the sauces and marinades that add flavor to barbecued foods.

RANCH PICNIC POTATO SALAD

6 medium potatoes (about 3½ pounds), cooked, peeled and sliced
½ cup chopped celery
¼ cup sliced green onions
2 tablespoons chopped parsley
¼ teaspoon salt
⅛ teaspoon black pepper
1 tablespoon Dijon-style mustard
1 cup prepared HIDDEN VALLEY RANCH® Original Ranch® Salad Dressing
2 hard-cooked eggs, finely chopped
Paprika
Lettuce (optional)

In large bowl, combine potatoes, celery, onions, parsley, salt and pepper. In small bowl, stir mustard into salad dressing; pour over potatoes and toss lightly. Cover and refrigerate several hours. Sprinkle with eggs and paprika. Serve in lettuce-lined bowl, if desired.

Makes 8 servings

CALIFORNIA SALAD

1 DOLE® Fresh Pineapple
1 head DOLE® Iceberg Lettuce
2 DOLE® Bananas, peeled, sliced
8 ounces seedless DOLE® Grapes
2 DOLE® Carrots, sliced
1 tomato, cut into wedges
½ cucumber, sliced
2 stalks DOLE® Celery, sliced
¼ cup DOLE® Whole Natural Almonds, toasted
Date Dressing (recipe follows)

Twist crown from pineapple. Cut pineapple lengthwise into quarters. Remove fruit with curved knife. Trim off core and cut fruit into thin wedges. Line serving platter with lettuce leaves. Arrange half the pineapple and remaining fruits and vegetables on lettuce. Reserve remaining pineapple for another use. Sprinkle with almonds. Serve with Date Dressing. *Makes 6 servings*

Date Dressing: In 1-quart measure, combine ⅔ cup vegetable oil, ¼ cup raspberry vinegar, 1 tablespoon sugar, 2 teaspoons soy sauce, 1 teaspoon *each* curry powder and dry mustard and ½ teaspoon garlic salt. Stir in ⅓ cup DOLE® Chopped Dates.

Top to bottom: Ranch Picnic Potato Salad, California Salad

FRUIT SALAD WITH ORANGE-ALMOND DRESSING

1 head DOLE® Leaf Lettuce
½ DOLE® Cantaloupe, cut into chunks
2 cups DOLE® Fresh Pineapple chunks
1 cup sliced DOLE® Strawberries
1 cup seedless DOLE® Grapes
1 DOLE® Orange, peeled and sectioned
1 DOLE® Peach, sliced
½ cup DOLE® Whole Natural Almonds, toasted
  Orange-Almond Dressing (recipe follows)

Line large salad bowl with lettuce leaves. Arrange fruit on top; sprinkle with almonds. Serve with Orange-Almond Dressing.

Makes 6 to 8 servings

Orange-Almond Dressing: In 1-quart measure, combine 1 cup dairy sour cream, ½ cup mayonnaise, ¼ cup toasted DOLE® Chopped Natural Almonds, 2 tablespoons lemon juice and 2 teaspoons grated DOLE® Orange peel. Refrigerate, covered, until ready to serve.

COOL AND CREAMY FRUIT SALAD

1 (8-ounce) package PHILADELPHIA BRAND® Cream Cheese, softened
2 tablespoons lemon juice
1 teaspoon grated lemon peel
1 cup thawed COOL WHIP® Whipped Topping
2 cups peach slices
2 cups blueberries
2 cups strawberry slices
2 cups grapes
2 tablespoons chopped nuts

Combine cream cheese, juice and peel, mixing until well blended. Fold in whipped topping; chill. Layer fruit in 2½-quart serving bowl. Top with cream cheese mixture and nuts. Chill.

Makes 8 servings

Variation: Substitute Light PHILADELPHIA BRAND® Neufchâtel Cheese for Cream Cheese.

SPARKLING BERRY SALAD

2 envelopes KNOX® Unflavored Gelatine
2 cups cranberry-raspberry juice, divided
⅓ cup sugar
1 cup club soda
¼ cup creme de cassis (black currant) liqueur (optional)
1 teaspoon lemon juice
1 teaspoon fresh grated orange peel (optional)
3 cups assorted blueberries, raspberries or strawberries
  Sour cream (optional)

In medium saucepan, sprinkle unflavored gelatine over 1 cup cranberry-raspberry juice; let stand 1 minute. Stir over low heat until gelatine is completely dissolved, about 5 minutes. Stir in sugar until dissolved.

In large bowl, blend remaining 1 cup cranberry-raspberry juice, soda, gelatine mixture, liqueur, lemon juice and orange peel. Chill, stirring occasionally, until mixture is consistency of unbeaten egg whites, about 60 minutes. Fold in berries. Pour into 6-cup mold or bowl; chill until firm, about 3 hours. Unmold and serve, if desired, with sour cream.

Makes about 8 servings

Fruit Salad with Orange-Almond Dressing

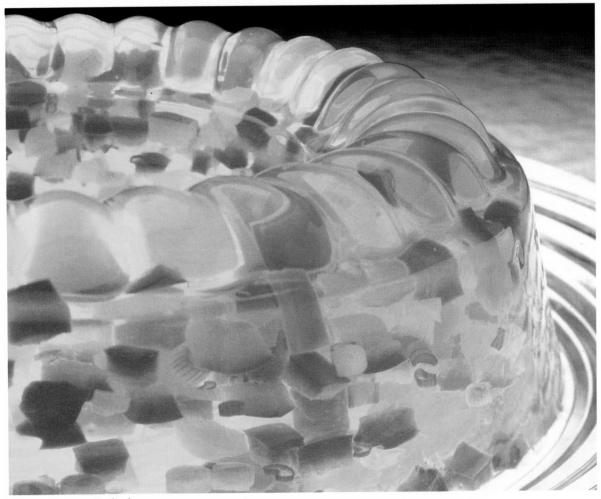

Three Pepper Salad

THREE PEPPER SALAD

   2 packages (4-serving size each) *or*
      1 package (8-serving size) JELL-O®
      Brand Gelatin, Lemon Flavor
   2 cups boiling water
1½ cups cold water
   2 tablespoons lemon juice
   2 cups chopped red, green and/or yellow
      peppers
   2 tablespoons sliced scallions
   Salsa Dressing (recipe follows) (optional)

Dissolve gelatin in boiling water. Stir in cold
water and lemon juice. Chill until thickened.
Fold in peppers and scallions. Pour gelatin
mixture into 5-cup mold. Chill until firm,
about 4 hours. Unmold. Cut into slices; serve
with Salsa Dressing, if desired.

Makes 10 servings

SALSA DRESSING
   ½ cup MIRACLE WHIP® Salad Dressing
   ½ cup sour cream
   ½ cup prepared salsa

Mix together ingredients until well blended.
Chill.   *Makes 1½ cups*

TANGY HONEY SAUCE

   1 cup catsup
   ¼ cup honey
   1 tablespoon prepared mustard
   ½ teaspoon ground nutmeg

Combine all ingredients; mix thoroughly.
Makes 1¼ cups

Serving Tip: Spread on meatloaf, pork loin,
ribs or chicken pieces during last 15 minutes of
baking or serve as dipping sauce.

*Favorite Recipe from **National Honey Board***

Classic Spinach Salad

CLASSIC SPINACH SALAD

- ½ pound fresh spinach leaves (about 10 cups)
- 1 cup sliced mushrooms
- 1 medium tomato, cut into wedges
- ⅓ cup seasoned croutons
- ¼ cup chopped red onion
- 4 slices bacon, crisp-cooked and crumbled
- ½ cup WISH-BONE® Lite Classic Dijon Vinaigrette Dressing
- 1 hard-cooked egg, sliced

In large salad bowl, combine spinach, mushrooms, tomato, croutons, red onion and bacon. Add lite classic Dijon vinaigrette dressing and toss gently. Garnish with egg.

Makes about 6 side-dish servings

DOLE® SUMMER VEGETABLE SALAD

- 1 head DOLE® Lettuce
- 2 tomatoes
- 1 cucumber
- ½ DOLE® Red Bell Pepper
- ¼ DOLE® Red Onion
- 1 cup sliced DOLE® Celery
- 1 cup snow peas, ends and strings removed
- 1 cup sliced DOLE® Cauliflower
- Dill Dressing (recipe follows)

Tear lettuce into bite-size pieces. Cut tomatoes into wedges. Slice cucumber, red pepper and red onion. Toss all vegetables in salad bowl with Dill Dressing. *Makes 4 servings*

Dill Dressing: In 1-quart measure, combine ½ cup *each* dairy sour cream and mayonnaise, 1 tablespoon vinegar, 1 teaspoon *each* dried dill weed and onion powder, 1 teaspoon Dijon-style mustard, ¾ teaspoon garlic salt and cracked pepper to taste. Refrigerate, covered, until ready to serve.

BARLEY WITH CORN AND RED PEPPER

½ cup WISH-BONE® Italian Dressing*
1 medium red pepper, chopped
½ cup chopped onion
1 cup uncooked pearled barley
1¾ cups chicken broth
1¼ cups water
2 tablespoons finely chopped coriander (cilantro) or parsley
1 tablespoon lime juice
½ teaspoon ground cumin
⅛ teaspoon pepper
1 can (7 ounces) whole kernel corn, drained

In large saucepan, heat Italian dressing; add red pepper and onion. Cook over medium heat, stirring occasionally, 5 minutes or until tender. Stir in barley and cook, stirring constantly, 1 minute. Stir in broth, water, coriander, lime juice, cumin and pepper. Simmer covered 50 minutes or until barley is done. (Do not stir while simmering.) Stir in corn. *Makes about 6 servings*

*Also terrific with WISH-BONE® Robusto Italian, Herbal Italian, Lite Italian, Blended Italian or Lite Classic Dijon Vinaigrette Dressing.

Country Cole Slaw

COUNTRY COLE SLAW

1 cup HELLMANN'S® or BEST FOODS® Real, Light or Cholesterol Free Reduced Calorie Mayonnaise
3 tablespoons lemon juice
2 tablespoons sugar
1 teaspoon salt
6 cups shredded cabbage
1 cup shredded carrots
½ cup chopped or thinly sliced green pepper

In medium bowl, combine mayonnaise, lemon juice, sugar and salt. Stir in cabbage, carrots and green pepper. Cover; chill.
Makes about 10 servings

RAITA
(Cucumber and Yogurt Salad)

3 medium cucumbers, peeled, seeded and thinly sliced
1 tablespoon minced onion
2 cups plain yogurt
½ teaspoon pepper
¼ teaspoon cumin
2 tablespoons cilantro, chopped

Mix together all ingredients. Chill for 2 to 24 hours to develop flavors.
Makes 4 to 6 servings

*Favorite Recipe from the **National Pork Producers Council***

Barley with Corn and Red Pepper

EASY MACARONI SALAD

1 cup HELLMANN'S® or BEST FOODS®
 Real, Light or Cholesterol Free
 Reduced Calorie Mayonnaise
2 tablespoons vinegar
1 tablespoon prepared yellow mustard
1 teaspoon sugar
1 teaspoon salt
¼ teaspoon freshly ground black pepper
8 ounces elbow macaroni, cooked, rinsed
 with cold water and drained
1 cup sliced celery
1 cup chopped green or red bell pepper
¼ cup chopped onion

In large bowl, combine mayonnaise, vinegar, mustard, sugar, salt and black pepper. Add macaroni, celery, green pepper and onion; toss to coat well. Cover; chill. Garnish as desired.

Makes about 8 servings

Note: If desired, stir in milk for a creamier salad.

CREAMY ITALIAN PASTA SALAD

1 cup HELLMANN'S® or BEST FOODS®
 Real, Light or Cholesterol Free
 Reduced Calorie Mayonnaise
2 tablespoons red wine vinegar
1 clove garlic, minced
1 tablespoon chopped fresh basil *or*
 1 teaspoon dried basil leaves
1 teaspoon salt
¼ teaspoon freshly ground black pepper
1½ cups twist or spiral pasta, cooked, rinsed
 with cold water and drained
1 cup quartered cherry tomatoes
½ cup coarsely chopped green pepper
½ cup slivered pitted ripe olives

In large bowl, combine mayonnaise, vinegar, garlic, basil, salt and pepper. Stir in pasta, cherry tomatoes, green pepper and olives. Cover; chill. *Makes about 6 servings*

CRANBERRY-APPLE WALDORF

2 envelopes KNOX® Unflavored Gelatine
⅓ cup sugar
½ cup boiling water
3½ cups cranberry juice cocktail
1 cup chopped apple
½ cup chopped celery
⅓ cup chopped walnuts
 Lettuce (optional)

In large bowl, mix unflavored gelatine with sugar; add boiling water and stir until gelatine is completely dissolved, about 5 minutes. Stir in cranberry juice. Chill, stirring occasionally, until mixture is consistency of unbeaten egg whites, about 45 minutes. Fold in remaining ingredients. Pour into 8-inch square baking pan; chill until firm, about 3 hours. To serve, cut into 4-inch squares and serve, if desired, on lettuce-lined plates.

Makes about 4 servings

GRAPES AND SPINACH SALAD

 Chutney Dressing (recipe follows)
1 pound spinach, washed, drained
1 cup California seedless grapes
1 apple, cored and diced
⅓ cup dry roasted peanuts
2 tablespoons chopped green onion
1 tablespoon toasted sesame seeds

Prepare Chutney Dressing. Tear spinach into bite-size pieces. Toss with grapes, apple, peanuts, green onion and sesame seeds in bowl. Toss with Chutney Dressing to coat well.

Makes 6 servings

Chutney Dressing: Combine 3 tablespoons vegetable oil, 2 tablespoons white wine vinegar, 1 tablespoon chopped chutney, ¼ teaspoon curry powder, ¼ teaspoon salt, ¼ teaspoon dry mustard and dash bottled hot pepper sauce in small bowl; mix well.

Makes about ⅓ cup

Favorite Recipe from California Table Grape Commission

Top to bottom: Easy Macaroni Salad,
Creamy Italian Pasta Salad

Top to bottom: Honey Almond Grilling Glaze, Onion-Molasses Barbecue Sauce

HONEY ALMOND GRILLING GLAZE

11 tablespoons unsalted butter, in all
2 tablespoons all-purpose flour
1 cup slivered almonds
2 tablespoons CHEF PAUL
    PRUDHOMME'S SEAFOOD MAGIC®
1 cup chopped celery
1 cup honey
1 teaspoon grated fresh lemon peel
1 cup chicken stock or water
⅛ teaspoon ground nutmeg

In small saucepan over medium heat, melt 3 tablespoons of the butter. Whisk in flour until smooth, about 1 minute. Reserve.

In 10-inch skillet over high heat, melt remaining 8 tablespoons butter. When it comes to a hard sizzle, add almonds, Seafood Magic and celery. Cook, stirring frequently at first and constantly near end of cooking time, about 8 minutes or until almonds are browned. Stir in honey and cook, stirring frequently, about 1 minute. Stir in lemon peel and stock. Cook, stirring occasionally, about 8 minutes. Add nutmeg; cook 3 minutes, stirring occasionally. Whisk in reserved butter mixture until it is incorporated and sauce is slightly thickened, 30 to 60 seconds. Remove from heat.

Makes about 2½ cups

Note: This glaze is wonderful on grilled seafood, chicken and pork. Brush it on right before meat is ready to come off the grill and bring some to the table for dipping.

ONION-MOLASSES BARBECUE SAUCE

4 tablespoons margarine
2 tablespoons walnut or vegetable oil
2 tablespoons olive oil
3 cups chopped onions
3 tablespoons CHEF PAUL
    PRUDHOMME'S POULTRY MAGIC®
¾ cup light molasses
1 cup cider vinegar
¼ cup freshly squeezed orange juice
½ teaspoon dried dill weed
½ cup chicken stock or water

In 10-inch skillet over high heat, melt margarine with walnut oil and olive oil. When it comes to a hard sizzle, add onions and Poultry Magic. Stir to mix well and cook, stirring frequently, about 8 minutes or until onions are browned. Stir in molasses, mixing well. Add vinegar, orange juice and dill weed. Stir well and cook about 12 minutes, stirring frequently. Stir in stock and cook about 2 minutes more for flavors to blend.

Makes about 3 cups

Note: This sauce was created for anything that can be grilled. Just mop it on generously near the end of cooking time.

ORANGE-BERRY SALAD

½ cup prepared HIDDEN VALLEY
    RANCH® Original Ranch® Salad
    Dressing
2 tablespoons orange juice
1 teaspoon grated orange peel
½ cup heavy cream, whipped
1 can (11 ounces) mandarin orange
    segments
2 packages (3 ounces each) strawberry- or
    raspberry-flavored gelatin
1 can (16 ounces) whole-berry cranberry
    sauce
½ cup walnut pieces
    Mint sprigs
    Whole fresh strawberries and
    raspberries

In large bowl, whisk together salad dressing,
orange juice and peel. Fold in whipped cream;
cover and refrigerate. Drain oranges, reserving
juice. Add water to juice to measure 3 cups;
pour into large saucepan and bring to boil. Stir
in gelatin until dissolved. Cover and refrigerate
until partially set. Fold orange segments,
cranberry sauce and walnuts into gelatin. Pour
into lightly oiled 6-cup ring mold. Cover and
refrigerate until firm; unmold. Garnish with
mint and fresh strawberries and raspberries.
Serve with chilled dressing.

Makes 8 servings

Orange-Berry Salad

THREE BEAN RICE SALAD

1 can (16 ounces) cut wax beans, drained
1 can (16 ounces) French-style green
    beans, drained
1 can (8¾ ounces) red kidney beans,
    drained
½ cup prepared GOOD SEASONS® Italian
    Salad Dressing
¼ cup thinly sliced onion rings
1 teaspoon salt
⅛ teaspoon pepper
1½ cups water
1½ cups Original MINUTE® Rice or
    MINUTE® Premium Long Grain Rice
    Lettuce

Mix beans, salad dressing, onion, ½ teaspoon
of the salt and the pepper in large bowl; set
aside to allow flavors to blend.

Meanwhile, bring water and remaining
½ teaspoon salt to a full boil in medium
saucepan. Stir in rice. Cover; remove from
heat. Let stand 5 minutes. Fold rice into bean
mixture. Cover and chill thoroughly. Serve on
lettuce.   *Makes 6 servings*

VERSATILE BARBECUE SAUCE

¼ cup chopped onion
1 clove garlic, finely chopped
2 tablespoons margarine or butter
1 cup ketchup
⅓ cup firmly packed brown sugar
¼ cup REALEMON® Lemon Juice from
    Concentrate
1 tablespoon Worcestershire sauce
2 teaspoons WYLER'S® or STEERO®
    Beef- or Chicken-Flavor Instant
    Bouillon *or* 2 Beef- or Chicken-Flavor
    Bouillon Cubes
1 teaspoon prepared mustard

In small saucepan, cook onion and garlic in
margarine until tender. Add remaining
ingredients; bring to a boil. Reduce heat;
simmer uncovered 20 minutes, stirring
occasionally. Use as a basting sauce for beef,
chicken or pork. Refrigerate leftovers.
                    Makes about 1½ cups

To microwave: In 1-quart glass measure, melt
margarine on 100% power (high) 30 to
45 seconds. Add onion and garlic; cook on
100% power (high) 1½ to 2 minutes or until
tender. Add remaining ingredients. Cook
loosely covered on 100% power (high) 3 to
5 minutes or until mixture boils; stir. Reduce
to 50% power (medium); cook covered 4 to
5 minutes to blend flavors.

CLASSIC WALDORF SALAD

½ cup HELLMANN'S® or BEST FOODS®
    Real, Light or Cholesterol Free
    Reduced Calorie Mayonnaise
1 tablespoon sugar
1 tablespoon lemon juice
⅛ teaspoon salt
3 medium-size red apples, cored and diced
1 cup sliced celery
½ cup chopped walnuts

In medium bowl, combine mayonnaise, sugar,
lemon juice and salt. Add apples and celery;
toss to coat well. Cover; chill. Just before
serving, sprinkle with walnuts.
                    Makes about 8 servings

Three Bean Rice Salad

VINAIGRETTE MARINADE

⅓ cup vegetable oil
⅓ cup sliced green onions
¼ cup REALEMON® Lemon Juice from
   Concentrate
5 teaspoons Dijon-style mustard
1½ teaspoons WYLER'S® or STEERO®
   Chicken- or Beef-Flavor Instant
   Bouillon
1 teaspoon sugar
¼ teaspoon garlic powder

In shallow dish or plastic bag, combine
ingredients; add chicken, beef, pork or fish.
Cover; marinate in refrigerator 4 hours or
overnight, turning occasionally. Remove meat
from marinade; grill or broil as desired, basting
frequently with marinade. Refrigerate leftover
meat.   *Makes about ¾ cup*

MEXICAN COLESLAW SALAD

1 envelope KNOX® Unflavored Gelatine
1 cup cold water
1 pint (16 ounces) sour cream
½ cup mayonnaise
2 cups shredded and coarsely chopped red
   or green cabbage
1 medium tomato, seeded and coarsely
   chopped
2 green onions, chopped (about ¼ cup)
2 tablespoons finely chopped coriander
   (cilantro) or parsley
1 tablespoon chili powder
1 tablespoon lime juice
1 teaspoon salt
½ teaspoon ground cumin
⅛ teaspoon pepper
   Red or green cabbage leaves

In medium saucepan, sprinkle unflavored
gelatine over cold water; let stand 1 minute. Stir
over low heat until gelatine is completely
dissolved, about 5 minutes.

In large bowl, with wire whisk or rotary beater,
thoroughly blend gelatine mixture, sour cream
and mayonnaise. Stir in remaining ingredients
except cabbage leaves. Turn into 6-cup bowl
lined with cabbage leaves or 6-cup mold; chill
until firm, about 3 hours. Unmold onto serving
platter.   *Makes about 12 servings*

California Fruit Salad

CALIFORNIA FRUIT SALAD

¼ cup HELLMANN'S® or BEST FOODS®
   Real, Light or Cholesterol Free
   Reduced Calorie Mayonnaise
¼ cup sour cream
1 tablespoon honey
1 teaspoon lime juice
½ teaspoon grated lime peel
2 cantaloupes, cut into half crosswise and
   seeded
4 cups assorted fresh fruit (strawberries,
   blueberries, honeydew melon and
   cantaloupe)
½ cup (2 ounces) crumbled blue cheese

In medium bowl, combine mayonnaise, sour
cream, honey, lime juice and lime peel. Cover;
chill. To serve, fill each cantaloupe half with
1 cup mixed fresh fruit. Sprinkle each with
2 tablespoons blue cheese; top with
2 tablespoon dressing. Garnish as desired.
               Makes 4 servings

Tempting Treats

These desserts are a delightful ending to an outdoor meal—they also make terrific indoor snacks!

GIANT RAISIN-CHIP FRISBEES

    1 cup butter or margarine, softened
    1 cup packed brown sugar
    ½ cup granulated sugar
    2 eggs
    1 teaspoon vanilla
1½ cups all-purpose flour
    ¼ cup unsweetened cocoa
    1 teaspoon baking soda
    1 cup (6 ounces) semisweet chocolate chips
    ¾ cup raisins
    ¾ cup chopped walnuts

Preheat oven to 350°F. Line cookie sheets with parchment paper or lightly grease and dust with flour. Cream butter with sugars in large bowl. Add eggs and vanilla; beat until light. Combine flour, cocoa and baking soda in small bowl. Add to creamed mixture with chocolate chips, raisins and walnuts; stir until well blended. Scoop out about ½ cupful of dough for each cookie. Place on prepared cookie sheets, spacing about 5 inches apart. Using knife dipped in water, smooth balls of dough out to 3½ inches in diameter. Bake 10 to 12 minutes or until golden. Remove to wire rack to cool.   *Makes about 16 cookies*

RICH AND CREAMY PEACH ICE CREAM

    2 eggs*
    2 cups sugar
    ½ cup milk
    3 cups whipping cream
    6 large *or* 10 medium fresh California
        peaches, pitted, quartered

Beat eggs until foamy. Gradually beat in sugar until thick and lemon colored. Mix in milk and cream. Purée peaches in blender to measure 5 cups. Combine with egg mixture in ice cream container. Prepare in ice cream maker according to manufacturer's directions. Ice cream will not be solid but should be just holding its shape. Pack into freezing containers and freeze solid.   *Makes about 3 quarts*

Favorite Recipe from California Tree Fruit Agreement

*Use clean, uncracked eggs.

Left to right: Giant Raisin-Chip Frisbees, Rich and Creamy Peach Ice Cream

Hershey's Syrup Pie

HERSHEY'S SYRUP PIE

9-inch baked pastry shell *or* 8-inch
   (6 ounces) packaged graham cracker
   crumb crust
2 egg yolks
⅓ cup cornstarch
¼ teaspoon salt
1¾ cups milk
1 cup HERSHEY'S Syrup
1 teaspoon vanilla extract
   Syrup Whipped Topping (recipe follows)
   Fresh fruit

In medium microwave-safe bowl beat egg
yolks. Add cornstarch, salt, milk and syrup;
blend well. Microwave at MEDIUM-HIGH
(70%) 6 to 8 minutes, stirring every 2 minutes
with whisk, or until mixture is smooth and
very thick. Stir in vanilla. Pour into crust. Press
plastic wrap directly onto surface; chill several
hours or overnight. Garnish with Syrup
Whipped Topping and fresh fruit.

Makes 6 to 8 servings

Syrup Whipped Topping: In small mixer bowl
combine 1 cup chilled whipping cream, ½ cup
HERSHEY'S Syrup, 2 tablespoons powdered
sugar and ½ teaspoon vanilla extract. Beat just
until cream holds definite shape; do not
overbeat.   *Makes about 2¼ cups topping*

BROWNIE FRUIT PIZZA

1 (12.9- *or* 15-ounce) package fudge
   brownie mix
1 (8-ounce) package cream cheese,
   softened
1 (14-ounce) can EAGLE® Brand
   Sweetened Condensed Milk (NOT
   evaporated milk)
½ cup frozen pineapple or orange juice
   concentrate, thawed
1 teaspoon vanilla extract
   Assorted fresh or canned fruit
   (strawberries, bananas, kiwifruit,
   orange, pineapple, etc.)

Preheat oven to 350°. Prepare brownie mix as
package directs. On greased pizza pan or
baking sheet, spread batter into 12-inch circle.
Bake 15 to 20 minutes. Meanwhile, in small
mixer bowl, beat cheese until fluffy. Gradually
beat in sweetened condensed milk until
smooth. Stir in juice concentrate and vanilla.
Chill thoroughly. Just before serving, spoon
filling over cooled brownie crust. Arrange fruit
on top. Refrigerate leftovers.

Makes one 12-inch pizza

GRAPE YOGURT POPS

2 cups (1 pint) plain low-fat yogurt
1 can (6 ounces) frozen orange juice
   concentrate, partially thawed
⅓ cup sugar
8 (4 ounces each) waxed paper cups
2 cups red, green or blue/black California
   grapes, halved and seeded, if
   necessary
8 popsicle sticks

Combine yogurt, orange concentrate and sugar;
stir until concentrate melts and sugar is
dissolved. Pour into paper cups, dividing
evenly. Drop ¼ cup grapes into each cup.
Freeze until almost firm. Insert stick in center
of cup. Freeze until firm. If made ahead, wrap
each in plastic wrap to prevent dehydration. To
serve, peel off paper cup.

Makes 8 servings

Favorite Recipe from **California Table Grape Commission**

Beat-the-Heat Cheesecake

BEAT-THE-HEAT CHEESECAKE

Graham Cracker-Almond Crust (recipe
   follows)
 2 envelopes KNOX® Unflavored Gelatine
¾ cup sugar
 1 cup boiling water
 2 packages (8 ounces each) cream cheese,
   softened
 1 cup (8 ounces) creamed cottage cheese
 1 cup (½ pint) whipping or heavy cream
 1 tablespoon vanilla extract
 1 tablespoon fresh grated lemon peel
   (optional)
   Fruit for garnish (optional)

Prepare Graham Cracker-Almond Crust. In
large bowl, mix unflavored gelatine with ¼ cup
sugar; add boiling water and stir until gelatine
is completely dissolved, about 5 minutes. With
electric mixer, add remaining ½ cup sugar,
cream cheese, cottage cheese, cream, vanilla
and lemon peel, one at a time, beating well
after each addition. Continue beating an
additional 5 minutes or until mixture is
smooth. Turn into Graham Cracker-Almond
Crust; chill until firm, about 5 hours. Garnish
with fruit, if desired.

Makes about 12 servings

Graham Cracker-Almond Crust: In small
bowl, combine 1 cup graham cracker crumbs,
½ cup ground almonds, 2 tablespoons sugar,
¼ cup melted butter or margarine and
½ teaspoon almond extract. Press onto bottom
and side of 9-inch springform pan; chill.

PEACH MELBA DESSERT

1 package (4-serving size) JELL-O® Brand
    Gelatin, Peach Flavor
2 cups boiling water
¾ cup cold water
1 package (4-serving size) JELL-O® Brand
    Gelatin, Raspberry Flavor
1 pint vanilla ice cream, softened
1 can (8¾ ounces) sliced peaches,
    drained*
½ cup fresh raspberries
    Mint leaves (optional)

Dissolve peach flavor gelatin in 1 cup of the boiling water. Add cold water. Chill until slightly thickened.

Dissolve raspberry flavor gelatin in remaining 1 cup boiling water. Spoon in ice cream, stirring until melted and smooth. Pour into serving bowl. Chill until set but not firm.

Arrange peach slices and raspberries on ice cream mixture in bowl. Add mint leaves, if desired. Spoon peach gelatin over fruit. Chill until firm, about 3 hours.

Makes 10 servings

*1 fresh peach, peeled and sliced, may be substituted for canned peaches.

Peach Melba Dessert

HONEY BERRY SAUCE

1 cup *each* frozen blackberries,
blueberries and raspberries
¾ cup cranberry juice
¼ cup honey
1½ teaspoons grated orange peel

Combine berries and thaw; drain and reserve
½ cup liquid. Combine cranberry juice,
reserved liquid and honey in small saucepan;
bring to boil over high heat. Reduce heat to
medium; simmer about 10 minutes or until
mixture is reduced to 1 cup. Remove from
heat; stir in orange peel. Cool; pour over
berries. Chill until serving time. Spoon over
ice cream or fruit sherbet.   *Makes 3 cups*

Storage Tip: Refrigerate in covered container
up to 1 week.

*Favorite Recipe from **National Honey Board***

BANANA FUDGE POPS

1 ripe, medium banana
1½ cups orange-banana juice
½ cup sugar
¼ cup HERSHEY'S Cocoa
1 can (5 ounces) evaporated milk
6 paper cold drink cups (5 ounces each)
6 wooden popsicle sticks

Slice banana into blender container; add juice.
Cover; blend until smooth. Add sugar and
cocoa; cover and blend well. Add evaporated
milk; cover and blend. Pour mixture into cups.
Freeze about 1 hour; insert popsicle sticks into
fudge pops. Cover; freeze until firm. Peel off
cups to serve.   *Makes 6 pops*

ICE CREAM COOKIES

2 squares (1 ounce each) unsweetened
chocolate
1 cup butter, softened
1 cup powdered sugar
4 egg yolks
1 teaspoon vanilla
3 cups all-purpose flour
Powdered sugar

Ice Cream Cookie Sandwiches

Melt chocolate in top of double boiler over hot,
not boiling, water. Remove from heat; cool.
Cream butter and 1 cup sugar in large bowl
until blended. Add egg yolks, vanilla and
melted chocolate; beat until light. Blend in
flour to make stiff dough. Divide dough into
4 parts. Shape each part into a roll, about
1½ inches in diameter. Wrap in plastic wrap;
refrigerate until firm, at least 30 minutes or up
to 2 weeks. (For longer storage, freeze up to
6 weeks.)

Preheat oven to 350°F. Line cookie sheets with
parchment paper or leave ungreased. Cut rolls
into ⅛-inch-thick slices; place 2 inches apart
on ungreased cookie sheets. Bake 8 to
10 minutes or just until set, but not browned.
Remove to wire racks to cool. Dust with
powdered sugar.

Makes about 8 dozen cookies

Ice Cream Cookie Sandwiches: Prepare and
bake cookies as directed; cool completely.
Spread desired amount of softened ice cream
on bottoms of half the cookies. Top with
remaining cookies, bottom sides down,
forming sandwiches. Dust tops with powdered
sugar; serve immediately.

Makes about 4 dozen sandwich cookies

Berried Delight

BERRIED DELIGHT

1½ cups graham cracker crumbs
½ cup sugar
⅓ cup PARKAY® Margarine, melted
1 package (8 ounces) PHILADELPHIA
    BRAND® Cream Cheese, softened
2⅔ cups cold milk
3½ cups (8 ounces) COOL WHIP® Whipped
    Topping, thawed
2 pints strawberries, hulled and halved
1 package (6-serving size) JELL-O®
    Instant Pudding and Pie Filling,
    French Vanilla or Vanilla Flavor

Combine crumbs and ¼ cup of the sugar. Mix
in margarine. Press mixture evenly onto
bottom of 13×9-inch pan. (If desired, bake at
375°F for 8 minutes. Cool on rack.)

Beat cream cheese with remaining ¼ cup
sugar and 2 tablespoons of the milk until
smooth. Fold in ½ of the whipped topping.
Spread over crust. Arrange strawberries in
even layer on cream cheese mixture.

Pour remaining milk into medium bowl. Add
pudding mix. Beat with wire whisk until well
blended, 1 to 2 minutes. Pour over
strawberries. Chill 4 hours or overnight.

Spread remaining whipped topping over
pudding just before serving. Garnish with
additional strawberries, if desired.
                    Makes 18 servings

FRESH STRAWBERRY PIE

1 (9-inch) baked pastry shell
1¼ cups sugar
1 tablespoon cornstarch
1½ cups water
3 tablespoons REALEMON® Lemon Juice
    from Concentrate
1 (4-serving size) package strawberry
    flavor gelatin
1 quart fresh strawberries, cleaned and
    hulled (about 1½ pounds)

In medium saucepan, combine sugar and
cornstarch; add water and ReaLemon® brand.
Over high heat, bring to a boil. Reduce heat;
cook, stirring occasionally, until slightly
thickened and clear, 4 to 5 minutes. Add
gelatin; stir until dissolved. Chill until
thickened but not set, about 1 hour. Stir in
strawberries; spoon into prepared pastry shell.
Chill 4 to 6 hours or until set. Refrigerate
leftovers.   *Makes one 9-inch pie*

To microwave: In 2-quart glass measure,
combine sugar and cornstarch; add water and
ReaLemon® brand. Cook on 100% power (high)
6 to 8 minutes, or until slightly thickened and
bubbly, stirring every 2 minutes. Proceed as
above.

Fresh Strawberry Pie

PEACH SURPRISE PIE

2 (8-ounce) packages PHILADELPHIA
    BRAND® "Light" Neufchâtel Cheese,
    softened
¼ cup sugar
½ teaspoon vanilla
    Pastry for 1-crust 9-inch pie, baked
1 (16-ounce) can peach slices, drained
¼ cup KRAFT® Red Raspberry Preserves
1 teaspoon lemon juice
    Fresh mint (optional)

Combine neufchâtel cheese, sugar and vanilla,
mixing until well blended. Spread onto bottom
of crust; chill several hours or overnight. Top
with peaches just before serving. Combine
preserves and juice, mixing until well blended.
Spoon over peaches. Garnish with fresh mint,
if desired.   *Makes 6 to 8 servings*

AMBROSIA

1 can (20 ounces) DOLE® Pineapple
    Chunks in Juice
1 can (11 ounces) DOLE® Mandarin
    Orange Segments in Syrup
1 firm, large DOLE® Banana, peeled,
    sliced (optional)
1½ cups seedless DOLE® Grapes
1 cup miniature marshmallows
1 cup flaked coconut
½ cup pecan halves or coarsely chopped
    nuts
1 cup dairy sour cream or plain yogurt
1 tablespoon brown sugar

Drain pineapple and orange segments. In large
bowl, combine pineapple, orange segments,
banana, grapes, marshmallows, coconut and
nuts. In 1-quart measure, combine sour cream
and brown sugar. Stir into fruit mixture.
Refrigerate, covered, 1 hour or overnight.
                            Makes 4 servings

Creamy Orange Mold

CREAMY ORANGE MOLD

2 packages (4-serving size each) *or*
    1 package (8-serving size)
    JELL-O® Brand Gelatin, Orange
    Flavor
2 cups boiling water
1 pint vanilla ice cream, softened
¾ cup orange juice
    Orange slices (optional)
    Strawberry halves (optional)
    Mint leaves (optional)

Dissolve gelatin in boiling water. Spoon in ice
cream, stirring until melted and smooth. Stir in
orange juice. Pour into 5-cup mold. Chill until
firm, about 4 hours. Unmold. Garnish with
orange slices, strawberry halves and mint
leaves, if desired.   *Makes 10 servings*

Refreshing Coolers

The coolers, mocktails and cocktails featured here are wonderful for sipping during a relaxing summer afternoon or evening.

THE MAIDEN MARY

2½ cups Florida grapefruit juice
2 cups tomato juice
1 cup clam juice
2 teaspoons Worcestershire sauce
Dash hot pepper sauce
Ice cubes

In 2-quart pitcher, combine grapefruit juice, tomato juice, clam juice, Worcestershire and hot pepper sauce; blend well. Add ice cubes. Pour into serving glasses. Garnish as desired.

Makes 4 servings

Favorite Recipe from Florida Department of Citrus

ORANGE FANTASIA

1½ cups Florida orange juice
1 cup (½ pint) orange sherbet
Cracked ice (optional)

Pour orange juice into blender container; add orange sherbet. Cover and process at medium speed until smooth. Or, sherbet may be softened slightly, added to orange juice and beaten with rotary beater until smooth. If desired, pour over cracked ice. Garnish as desired. *Makes 2½ cups or 2 servings*

Favorite Recipe from Florida Department of Citrus

LEMONADE

½ cup sugar
½ cup REALEMON® Lemon Juice from Concentrate
3¼ cups cold water
Ice cubes

In large pitcher, dissolve sugar in ReaLemon® brand; add water. Serve over ice. Garnish as desired. *Makes about 1 quart*

Sparkling Lemonade: Substitute club soda for cold water.

Slushy Lemonade: In blender container, combine ReaLemon® brand and sugar with ½ cup water. Gradually add 4 cups ice cubes, blending until smooth. Serve immediately.

Pink Lemonade: Stir in 1 to 2 teaspoons grenadine syrup *or* 1 to 2 drops red food coloring.

Minted Lemonade: Stir in 2 to 3 drops peppermint extract.

Low Calorie: Omit sugar. Add 4 to 8 envelopes sugar substitute *or* 1½ teaspoons liquid sugar substitute.

Left to right: The Maiden Mary, Orange Fantasia, Lemonade

Top to bottom: Strawberry-Banana Shake, Banana Shake

BANANA SHAKE

2 ripe bananas, cut up (about 2 cups)
⅓ cup REALEMON® Lemon Juice from
   Concentrate
1 cup cold water
1 (14-ounce) can EAGLE® Brand
   Sweetened Condensed Milk (NOT
   evaporated milk)
2 cups ice cubes

In blender container, combine all ingredients except ice; blend well. Gradually add ice; blend until smooth. Garnish as desired. Refrigerate leftovers. (Mixture stays thick and creamy in refrigerator.)

Makes about 5 cups

Strawberry-Banana Shake: Reduce bananas to ½ cup; add 1½ cups fresh strawberries *or* 1 cup frozen unsweetened strawberries, partially thawed. Proceed as above.

Mixer Method: Omit ice cubes. In large mixer bowl, mash bananas; gradually beat in ReaLemon® brand, sweetened condensed milk and 2½ cups cold water. Chill before serving.

PINA COLADA MOCKTAIL

1 can (6 ounces) frozen limeade
   concentrate, thawed
6 cups DOLE® Pine-Passion-Banana Juice,
   chilled
2 bottles (28 ounces each) mineral water,
   chilled
1 can (15 ounces) real cream of coconut
   Lime slices for garnish
   DOLE® Orange slices for garnish
   Mint sprigs for garnish

Reconstitute limeade according to label directions in large punch bowl. Add remaining ingredients.   *Makes 24 servings*

MAI TAI SLUSH

1½ cups DOLE® Pineapple Juice
1 pint lemon sherbet
2 ounces rum
2 tablespoons triple sec
1 cup crushed ice
   Lime slices for garnish (optional)

Combine pineapple juice, sherbet, rum and triple sec in blender. Add ice; blend until slushy. Garnish with lime slices, if desired.

Makes 2 servings

Mai Tai Slush

Double Berry Coco Punch

DOUBLE BERRY COCO PUNCH

Ice Ring (recipe follows) (optional) *or* block of ice
2 (10-ounce) packages frozen strawberries in syrup, thawed
1 (15-ounce) can COCO LOPEZ® Cream of Coconut
1 (48-ounce) bottle cranberry juice cocktail, chilled
2 cups light rum (optional)
1 (32-ounce) bottle club soda, chilled

Prepare ice ring in advance, if desired. In blender container, purée strawberries and cream of coconut until smooth. In large punch bowl, combine strawberry mixture, cranberry juice and rum, if desired. Just before serving, add club soda and ice ring.

Ice Ring: Fill ring mold with water to within 1 inch of top rim; freeze. Arrange strawberries, cranberries, mint leaves, lime slices or other fruits on top of ice. Carefully pour small amount of cold water over fruits; freeze.

Makes about 4 quarts

ORANGE AND SPICE ICED TEA

6 cups cold water, divided
3 cinnamon sticks (2 inches each)
½ teaspoon whole cloves
10 tea bags
1 can (6 ounces) Florida frozen concentrated orange juice, thawed, undiluted
¼ cup sugar
1 Florida orange, sliced

In medium saucepan, combine 3 cups cold water, cinnamon sticks and cloves. Bring to boiling; remove from heat. Add tea bags. Brew 5 minutes. Remove tea bags; discard. Strain mixture. Add remaining 3 cups cold water, orange juice concentrate and sugar; mix well. Chill. Serve in tall glasses over ice cubes.

Garnish with fresh orange slices.

Makes six 8-ounce servings

*Favorite Recipe from **Florida Department of Citrus***

LEMONY LIGHT COOLER

3 cups dry white wine or white grape juice,
    chilled
½ to ¾ cup sugar
½ cup REALEMON® Lemon Juice from
    Concentrate
1 (32-ounce) bottle club soda, chilled
    Strawberry, plum, peach or orange slices
    or other fresh fruit

In pitcher, combine wine, sugar and
ReaLemon® brand; stir until sugar dissolves.
Just before serving, add club soda and fruit;
serve over ice.   *Makes about 7 cups*

Tip: Recipe can be doubled.

Left to right: City Slicker, The Rattlesnake

CITY SLICKER

¾ cup DOLE® Pineapple Juice
    Ice cubes
    Ginger ale
    Dash ground ginger
    Cucumber slice, cherry tomato and
      lemon slice for garnish

Pour pineapple juice over ice cubes in glass.
Fill with ginger ale. Add ginger and stir.
Garnish with cucumber slice, cherry tomato
and lemon slice.   *Makes 1 serving*

THE RATTLESNAKE

3 cups DOLE® Pineapple Juice
⅓ cup tomato juice
1 tablespoon powdered sugar
½ to 1 teaspoon liquid hot pepper sauce
8 ice cubes
    Lime wedges or slices (optional)
    Dried red pepper, ripe olive and lime
      peel for garnish

In pitcher, combine pineapple juice, tomato
juice, sugar and hot pepper sauce; blend well.
Pour over ice cubes in glass. Squeeze lime
juice into each drink, if desired. Garnish with
dried red pepper, ripe olive and lime peel.
    Makes 4 servings

Lemony Light Cooler

LITE QUENCHER

3 cups DOLE® Pineapple Juice, chilled
3 cups mineral water, chilled
1 cup assorted sliced DOLE® fresh fruit
½ cup mint sprigs
1 lime, sliced, for garnish

Combine all ingredients in pitcher.

Makes 8 servings

APPLE GRAPE PUNCH

Ice Ring (recipe follows) (optional) *or*
    block of ice
1 quart apple juice, chilled
3 cups red grape juice, chilled
1 (8-ounce) bottle REALIME® Lime Juice
    from Concentrate, chilled
1 cup vodka (optional)
½ cup sugar

Prepare ice ring in advance, if desired. In punch bowl, combine juices, vodka, if desired, and sugar; stir until sugar dissolves. Just before serving, add ice ring.

Ice Ring: Combine 1 (8-ounce) bottle ReaLime® brand and ¾ cup sugar; stir until sugar dissolves. Add 3 cups water; mix well. Pour 3 cups mixture into ring mold; freeze. Arrange apple slices and grapes on top of ice. Carefully pour remaining mixture over fruits; freeze.   *Makes about 2 quarts*

Apple Grape Punch

Bloody Marys

BLOODY MARY

3 cups tomato juice, chilled
¾ cup vodka
4 teaspoons REALEMON® Lemon Juice
    from Concentrate
2 teaspoons Worcestershire sauce
½ teaspoon celery salt
⅛ teaspoon hot pepper sauce
    Dash pepper

In pitcher, combine ingredients; stir. Serve over ice; garnish as desired.

Makes about 1 quart

Tip: For nonalcoholic Bloody Mary, omit vodka. Proceed as above.

BLOODY MARY GARNISHES
Onion & Olive Pick: Dip cocktail onions in chopped parsley; alternate on toothpick with pimiento-stuffed olives.

Green Onion Firecracker: With small scissors or very sharp knife, cut tips of green onion to end of dark green onion portion. Chill in ice water until curled.

Top to bottom: Strawberry Margaritas, Frozen Margaritas

STRAWBERRY MARGARITAS

    1 (10-ounce) package frozen strawberries
       in syrup, partially thawed
¼ cup REALIME® Lime Juice from
       Concentrate
¼ cup tequila
¼ cup confectioners' sugar
    2 tablespoons triple sec or other orange-
       flavored liqueur
    3 cups ice cubes

In blender container, combine all ingredients except ice; blend well. Gradually add ice, blending until smooth. Garnish as desired. Serve immediately. *Makes about 1 quart*

FROZEN MARGARITAS

½ cup REALIME® Lime Juice from
       Concentrate
½ cup tequila
¼ cup triple sec or other orange-flavored
       liqueur
    1 cup confectioners' sugar
    4 cups ice cubes

In blender container, combine all ingredients except ice; blend well. Gradually add ice, blending until smooth. Garnish as desired. Serve immediately. *Makes about 1 quart*

PACIFIC SUNSET

    1 can (6 ounces) or ¾ cup DOLE®
       Pineapple Juice, chilled
⅓ cup orange juice, chilled
       Ice cubes
    1 tablespoon grenadine syrup
       Lime wedge for garnish

Combine juices in tall glass. Add ice. Slowly add grenadine. Garnish with lime wedge.
Makes 1 serving

STRAWBERRY LEMONADE

    1 quart fresh strawberries, cleaned and
       hulled (about 1½ pounds)
    3 cups cold water
¾ cup REALEMON® Lemon Juice from
       Concentrate
¾ to 1 cup sugar
    2 cups club soda, chilled
       Ice

In blender container, purée strawberries. In pitcher, combine puréed strawberries, water, ReaLemon® brand and sugar; stir until sugar dissolves. Add club soda. Serve over ice; garnish as desired. *Makes about 2 quarts*

Strawberry Lemonade

Acknowledgments

*The publishers would like to thank the
companies and organizations listed
below for the use of their recipes
in this book.*

Alaska Seafood Marketing Institute
Almond Board of California
American Lamb Council
Best Foods
Borden Kitchens, Borden, Inc.
California Table Grape Commission
California Tree Fruit Agreement
California Turkey Industry Board
Chef Paul Prudhomme's Magic Seasoning Blends™
Clear Springs Trout Company
Delmarva Poultry Industry, Inc.
Dole Food Company
Florida Department of Citrus
Florida Department of Natural Resources

©Hershey Foods Corporation
The HVR Company
The Kingsford Products Company
Kraft General Foods, Inc.
Lawry's Foods, Inc.
The Lipton Kitchens
McIlhenny Company, Avery Island, LA 70013
National Broiler Council
National Fisheries Institute
National Honey Board
National Live Stock and Meat Board
National Pork Producers Council
Perdue Farms Incorporated
StarKist Seafood Company
Swift-Eckrich, Inc.

Photo Credits

*The publishers would like to thank the
companies and organizations listed
below for the use of their photographs
in this book.*

Alaska Seafood Marketing Institute
Almond Board of California
American Lamb Council
Best Foods
Borden Kitchens, Borden, Inc.
California Turkey Industry Board
Chef Paul Prudhomme's Magic Seasoning Blends™
Clear Springs Trout Company
Dole Food Company
Florida Department of Natural Resources

©Hershey Foods Corporation
The HVR Company
The Kingsford Products Company
Kraft General Foods, Inc.
Lawry's Foods, Inc.
The Lipton Kitchens
National Live Stock and Meat Board
National Pork Producers Council
StarKist Seafood Company
Swift-Eckrich, Inc.

Index